The Nano Distillery
The Future of Distilling

Compiled by Bill Owens

Edited by Brad Plummer and Andrew Faulkner

White Mule Press a division of the
American Distilling Institute™

PO Box 577
Hayward, CA 94543
whitemulepress.com

ISBN 978-1-7322354-0-3

Front cover— Five 26-gallon Hillbilly Stills pot stills
finish all Lyon Distilling Company's spirits—from
rum to whiskey—at their distillery on the Eastern
Shore of Maryland.
© Jaime Windon

Back cover— A former gas station is reborn as a
distillery at Rowhouse Spirits in Philadelphia, PA,
© Bill Owens

Lee Spirits Co., Boulder, CO

Contents

Starting Distillery 291

Michael Myers, Distillery 291 [2017]

Whatever your definition of "nano distillery," going from grain to barrel to bottle, making 60 gallons a month in 339 sq. ft. certainly belongs in that category.

A typical day: I leaned over, pushed the button to the steam generator and watched the blue light wink on, then walked back to my makeshift desk to make notes. An hour later I heard a clunk. Little did I know that I would hear that clunk a few more times over the next few years.

The blue light was off, the still was warm and the steam trap was not spraying water, so I pushed the button again. The blue light returned, and hot water poured from the steam trap. It seemed everything was OK.

Returning to my desk, I thought about it a little and returned to making notes. Another hour later, I heard the clunk again, and thought, "Oh, there's an automatic off" on the home steam shower unit I was using as my steam generator.

Over the next two years, I reset that button more than 8,000 times.

The day was September 11, 2011, and it was the first run of DSP-CO-15023, the distilled spirits plant of Distillery 291 Colorado Whiskey. Our permit number DSP-CO-15023 means we are the 23rd DSP in the state.

It was a long way from my old life—of shooting the Olsen twins and hanging out in the SubMercer with Ivan Bart and Jimmy Fallon—to making 291 Colorado Whiskey in half of the basement of an old house commercially zoned on Tejon Street in Colorado Springs, Colorado.

A year earlier, in August 2010, on a flight back from NYC after a shoot for Vanity Fair, I read an article about Steven Grasse, the creator of Hendrick's Gin and Sailor Jerry. And I thought to myself, "Hey, I can do that." Stranahan's was in Denver, and I could take a tour and see what it was about. Returning to The Springs after the tour, I reached out to Mike Bristol of Bristol Brewing Company to ask his thoughts. He said, "Get your license and I'll try to help. I don't know much about distilling but I know how to brew."

As a photographer coming from the fashion and advertising world, I thought about buying whiskey and branding it until a friend at the time said I should make it. He encouraged me by saying if I couldn't make it, I could hire a distiller or buy the whiskey.

So, I set out to read all I could, the first book being Craft of Whiskey Distilling by Bill Owens, which talked about aligning a distillery with a brewery to save money on equipment and space. Again, I thought of Mike Bristol—he makes good beer. Maybe one of his would work. It's how Stranahan's started. Compass IPA was my first experiment. I learned hops can be a problem in distillate. Concentrated, they become very bitter and odd in flavor but I learned the still-ages had amazing aromas and flavor. Maybe using the stillage to mash back in would bring these flavors to the whiskey and add depth. I now call this process the El Paso County Process. Every mash gets a percentage of beer stillage mashed back in with grain and water. Working on a small scale allowed me to experiment without it being too expensive.

Acknowlegements

The American Distilling Institute was able to draw from its wide network of resources to bring this compilation to readers. Thanks to Andrew Faulkner and Brad Plummer for the many hours of editing, to Matt Kramer for copy editing, and to all the esteemed contributors: Philip Crossley (http://www.stilldragon.com), Steve Dalbey, Coleen Moore, Bess Morgan, Brad Plummer, Randy Pratt, Marc Sorini, Gary Spedding and Donald Snyder.

Part One
Getting Started

Bill Owens, president of the American Distilling Institute (ADI), has a standing offer: He will take anyone out to dinner who gets their distillery open in under two years. To date (2018), Bill reports he has received only four calls from distillers who say "they did it." (You can find Bill's phone number on the ADI website at www.distilling.com.)

One increasingly common path into the distilling business for those with minimal funding is to start by building a nano distillery. For the purposes of this book, a nano distillery is defined as one producing from 20 to 200 gallons a week. The emerging culture of nano distilleries is as diverse and varied as the ingenuity required to build one—elbow grease, sweat, sleepless nights, out-of-the-box thinking and clever workarounds are the coins of the realm when it comes to getting a safe and functional working distillery open on a shoestring budget. And make no mistake, they may be smaller in scale, but opening a nano distillery comes with its own enormous set of challenges. But it can also be a (relatively) inexpensive way to learn the ins and outs of pro ducing spirits commercially (as compared to the big shops). And it can be a great way to bootstrap your craft-spirits business ambitions into something larger.

Start by joining the American Distilling Institute (ADI). Members receive access to spreadsheets and business plans, as well as a subscription to *Distiller* magazine and access to the annual spirits conference. On the ADI website, you can also sign up for the weekly electronic newsletter and link to the ADI Forums (http://ADIforums.com). The forum discussion group is free and open to all—ask any question and someone with expertise will answer it. The forum has 40,000 visitors a month, and at any given moment there are 50 people online discussing distilling and spirits. It's an excellent resource to get acquainted with the practice and culture of craft distilling.

Building a library is also critical. This book is a good place to start. You can find a collection of useful and informative books on distilling and the craft-spirits business through White Mule Press (www.whitemulepress.com)—*The Distillers Guide to Rum, Craft of Whiskey Distilling, Traditional Distillation Art & Passion, The Maturation of Distilled Spirits: Vision and Patience, The Craft of Gin* and *Branding:Distilled* are all great guides to various aspects of the industry. All of these books can be found directly through ADI's publishing division, White Mule Press (www.whitemulepress.com), and at www.amazon.com. (And although most everyone will find the information presented in this book useful for building a nano distillery, most of the the regulatory information applies specifically to readers in the U.S. Always check the laws in your jurisdiction!)

Finally, spend some time visiting distilleries in your area and around the country if you can. Most give public tours, and the ones who don't are usually more than happy to host by appointment those interested in seeing the operation. Taste their products and ask questions. You can also find hands-on training opportunities through ADI, at the conference and throughout the year, to learn how to make just about anything that requires a still. But most importantly, do your homework. Craft distilling is a rewarding industry, but ask anyone who's made the leap and you will universally hear that it's probably the most challenging project they've ever jumped into. Read, ask, learn, take classes and take your time. Make sure you understand what you are really getting into when opening a distillery. With diligence and patience, it will be well worth your effort. Do it right and you just might find yourself across the table from Bill Owens.

—The American Distilling Institute, 2018

Chapter One

Ten Questions To Answer and Five Things To Do Before Opening A Distillery

Answer the following:

1. Why do I want to do this?

2. What are the federal, state and local laws regarding opening a distillery and producing distilled spirits? (What can I do and not do?) How long will it take to get licensed?

3. What products will I manufacture, and what equipment do I need to do it right?

4. What raw materials do I need to make these products, and where can I get them?

5. What kind of location do I need (consider zoning, building size, electrical requirements, plumbing, water source, etc.) and which local departments are involved in permitting? (Fire Department, City Planning, Environmental and Hazardous Materials Commission, etc.)

6. What will my brand be? What is the story? What makes my product unique? (Location? Technique? History? Source materials? etc.)

7. How much must I manufacture in the first year? How much can I reasonably sell? In subsequent years? What are my costs, and how much must I charge to make a sustainable profit? How long can I survive without any profit? And what happens when things go differently than planned?

8. How will I sell what I manufacture? (Self-distribute? Distributor? On-site? Bars, restaurants? Events? Online?)

9. Can I do this alone or do I need help? (Partners, lawyers, consultants, hourly workers, etc.)

10. After answering all of these, do I still want to open a distillery?

If the answer is YES to question 10:

1. Do your homework. Thoroughly research the market at the national and local levels: Who is doing what in this industry? What business models are working,? How do others do what they do? Explore the ADI forums, read books.

2. Visit other distilleries and take hands-on distilling classes. Ask lots of questions. About everything.

3. Make a detailed business plan, using real numbers. Get a second opinion from a business consultant to vet your assumptions around sales and cash flow, etc.

4. Raise the money needed, plus 20% more.

5. Apply for federal, state and local permits. OPEN & ENJOY!

Chapter Two

Just Do It—Or Get a Dog

by Randy Pratt, Owner and distiller, Great Notch Distillery

In 2012 I caught the "distilling fever." I attended workshops provided by the American Distilling Institute (ADI), met with various distillers and visited numerous distilleries near and far. I reached out to those in the know about the industry including ADI President Bill Owens. Bill's sage advice was three simple words, "Just do it." So, in consultation with my wife, I began my conversation with her by offering an option of either getting a dog or starting a distillery. My wife never thought I was serious enough to start a distillery and she wouldn't allow a dog in our home. I moved forward.

Now, let me tell you that when visiting distilleries, you're captivated by the romance of the finished product, bottled with a fancy label and prominently displayed. Your nose picks up the scent of fermentation and the aroma of feints coming off the still. The still itself is an attraction, all shiny and humming, as it produces the liquid of a mighty fine spirit. Barrels are photo-ready, lined up neatly on racks. Can you feel the romance charming you, enticing you to dive into the world of distilling? I was once told by a distiller, "If I can do it, anybody can do it."

Not so fast, mister. What he failed to tell me is that distilling was the only responsibility he had. He didn't do, and had no concern for, all the other things associated with a distillery.

I consider myself a well-educated man, with a Ph.D. and nearly 32 years in education as a teacher and school administrator, attaining the rank of superintendent. I was ready for a new challenge in my life. However, entering the world of craft distilling can be daunting, especially as a one-person operation. Here are some of the things I've learned in a short period of time.

Applying for a federal license wasn't the worst experience. Having been a school administrator, I was used to bureaucratic red tape. (Have you been to the DMV lately?) Happily, my federal permit was approved in less than four months.

My first real foray into the trials and tribulations began with state licensing. I don't know how your state works, but in mine (New Jersey), you are assigned a "case manager." This person receives your paperwork to review and notifies you of any necessary corrections or additional documentation. I learned early on to always send my paperwork via certified mail if a faxed or scanned copy wouldn't suffice. If it was faxed or scanned, I would keep the "transmission OK" sheet. Follow-up verification phone calls were received with annoyance. There were times when information was sent but those on the receiving end said they didn't receive it (i.e., they misplaced it). This pushed the approval back even farther.

And then there's the required site visit for final permit approval. Keep in mind that while you are waiting for your federal and state permits, you are paying rent, utilities and insurance on the space you are leasing. Sure, you can prepare your space for production and order all of your equipment, but you run the risk of spending money on something that might not happen.

An inspection date was scheduled, looking like state approval would be close at hand. Foolish me. The initial inspection didn't happen because the case manager forgot to write it in his calendar. Another date was canceled because of an ill child (understandable, it happens). Another time, I was told that the motor-pool car had to go in for service. On another date, the brakes needed to be replaced. Then the transmission. Then a department boss requested it for his or her use on another rescheduled day. At this point, weeks later, I offered to pick up and return the case manager using my car, which was declined by the department. By the time the site visit was made, weeks went by and the calendar changed another month, and I waited and waited. What should have taken two, maybe three months tops, took nearly eight months before the final permit was granted. I was five months behind my schedule and thousands of dollars out of pocket. To be fair, a craft distillery was a new concept at the time (having been approved in August 2013). So, everyone had a learning curve and could be given some slack. But don't think this slack will ever apply to you, so never be late with a report!

Lesson: Your time frame will not match with those who are assigned to you, regardless of how easy and organized you make it for them. Also, know that you will encounter different interpretations by different people in the same office. Have one person as your contact. And do not be afraid to ask for another opinion if you believe a response you receive is unnecessary, excessive or incorrect.

I received my state permit and, soon after, received a letter from my local municipal government. "Congratulations! You have received your State and Federal permits for distillation of beverage alcohol. By the way, our local ordinance does not allow you to provide tours, tastings, sell directly or provide a retail store on site."

What?! Gee, wouldn't it have been nice if this information had been furnished to me when I received my certificate of occupancy so many months earlier from the same issuing local authority? When questioned about this, the response was, "If we do it for you, we'll have to do it for everyone else in that development." This, my fellow and aspiring distillers, is a significant drawback. Customers and potential brand ambassadors can't tour, taste or purchase at the distillery to then disperse into the world wearing my logo t-shirt purchased from my retail store. So, as you decide on a location for your distillery, make sure you know the business activities allowed by your local authorities.

Now all the permits have been received and the distillery is a federally bonded facility. The locks have been changed to meet the Code of Federal Regulations (CFR). A few days later, I receive a certified letter from my landlord's attorney notifying me that I am hereby evicted because the landlord cannot get into the unit. What was openly and clearly discussed and agreed upon verbally before the lease-signing has now become tenuous and uncomfortable because limited access was never put in writing. After much haggling and hassle, with the real threat of eviction, I reached out to the TTB to structure language for approval as an addendum allowing specific restricted access to the distillery. This was eventually accepted, but left a sour taste in everyone's mouth in regard to trust.

Lesson: Get everything in writing, regardless of how small or petty you believe it to be. Check it and double-check it. Then have an attorney check it. Things will come up that you don't expect, and that once-friendly relationship between renter and landlord can sour quickly.

A few months later, I received another letter from another new distillery, reading: "Hey, you have the same fanciful label name as I have." My response: "Sorry, Mr. New Distillery, but I have formula approval, certificate of label approval (COLA), brand registration and product already made, bottled, labeled, boxed and on store shelves." "Oh, yeah," responded Mr. New Distillery, with a cease and desist letter. "I have trademark application before you. So there!" Damn. He's right. Now, I could fight this Mr. New Distillery, who has deep pockets, and spend my cash on an attorney. In my case, I decided to rebrand instead of fight. The name change actually worked in my favor, allowing for a better name, better design and better marketing.

The lesson here is that something like this can actually be a blessing. The TTB and COLA, as with other bureaucratic agencies, don't cross-communicate with the U.S. Patent and Trademark Office. Apply for trademark application before someone else takes your bright idea.

"Nobody buys vodka." "Nobody buys gin." "Nobody buys whiskey." Did I walk into a liquor store or a butcher shop? Having the ability to self-distribute is a wonderful thing. I meet really great people during sales calls. However, during one particular sales call, the person behind the counter couldn't have cared less that I am one of the few small craft distillers in the state and make wonderful local spirits for her consumers. In your sales efforts, you will encounter amazing forms of rejection. Whether you are self-distributing or trying to connect with a distributor, there is a 100% chance you will experience rejection. Regularly. If you are thin-skinned or have an inferior product, it will be even harder. Some people will nicely say they are not interested after your initial elevator speech, and you'll move on. Others will sample your products (because it's free booze) with no intent of ever placing an order. Others will find an excuse such as, "Oh. You only have 750s. We want 375s." Or even, "You're a small craft what? I didn't know a distillery made alcohol. It always comes in a bottle." (Seriously.)

The lesson here is that you can't please all of the people all of the time. But, you have to be at your best during sales calls because you never know what might spark a buyer's interest. It may not be on their shelf today, but maybe a month or a year from now it will be.

(Honestly though, it is difficult to self-distribute. It takes time away from distilling, daily operations, marketing and other essential matters. However, you do meet some fascinating people.)

As a small craft distiller and business owner still trying to find my way, I've learned that you can definitely expect things to happen along your journey that weren't in your business plan. Without fail: Equipment you order will arrive with missing parts. Supplies will be sent to the wrong address. Bottles will arrive broken or damaged. (Hint: Take the extra delivery insurance.) That phone call or email that you sent needing an answer yesterday won't be returned today or tomorrow. And get used to hearing: "You make booze? Can I have a free bottle or two? Can I have a free hat, t-shirt or sweatshirt?"

When visiting other distillers, be mindful of their time. It's not that we don't want to speak with you. We all take pride in the spirits we make. However, we just don't have the time in many cases to spend with you. We aren't afraid of you stealing trade secrets. (Well, maybe just a little.) Realize that everyone has their own journey of why and how they arrived at becoming a distiller. You will follow your own unique path. You will have bumps and bruises, just as we have. You will be making decisions and choices every day. Some easy, some not. These choices range from the color of your labels, the diameter size needed for the cork, type of still, where and from whom to purchase grain, where to set up shop, which insurance company to go with, to the type of flavor profile you want in your spirits. Your list will be extensive, tedious and never-ending.

You will receive endless emails and phone calls soliciting donations or participation in some function where you supply the alcohol. I try to limit the number of organizations and fund-raisers I attend. Everyone will tell you it's "good exposure for your brand." Maybe so, but it's also free alcohol for them and becomes a liability to you by giving away free booze. Regardless, do something nice and reasonable for a cause you believe in. During Memorial Day weekend, I donate a percentage of the wholesale sales to the Wounded Warrior Project because this organization, and the Make-A-Wish Foundation, are important to me. No matter how small your contribution, do something beneficial for others. You can then kick back with a glass of your perfectly distilled spirit and raise a toast to yourself for being so good.

If you aspire to open a distillery and have the patience, desire to learn, organizational skills and, of course, the cash, then the words of Bill Owens ring true: "Just do it." Or, in the words of my wife now, "We should have gotten two dogs.

Part Two
Regulations, Operations & Construction

Chapter Three

Seven Key Considerations for Designing a Nano Distillery

Colleen Moore, Director of Marketing and Operations,
Dalkita Architecture & Construction

Know the rules that apply to your facility.
Contact your local building department. Find out what year/version of the International Code Council (ICC), International Building Code (IBC) and International Fire Code (IFC) their rules are based on. They use these rules to review and approve architectural and engineering drawings.

Get a copy of the current code—some places offer it for free online, others tell you where you can purchase it. Be aware that some communities repackage the model codes from ICC, sometimes with revisions, as their own code. For instance, the Oregon Building Code and the Florida Building Code are both rooted in the model codes created by the ICC.

Get a current copy of the local amendments—things specific to your locality that have been added to or subtracted from to the International Codes to tailor the model codes to fit your community.

Hire a licensed architect with commercial (versus residential) experience. The vast majority of jurisdictions want accurate drawings and professional, stamped plans for complex and technical commercial jobs such as a distillery. The building and fire codes set a limit to the amount of combustible and flammable liquids allowed in your space. If your facility has no fire sprinklers—known as un-sprinkled—the Maximum Allowable Quantity (MAQ) of flammable liquids allowed in use or in closed process is 120 gallons at any one time (not counting finished, bottled product).

Sprinklers are strongly recommended—but not strictly required.
There are major benefits to spaces equipped with fire sprinklers—for instance, you can double the MAQ to 240 gallons—if the sprinklers meet the requirements of your fire department and the National Fire Protection Association.

There is little to no premium or additional cost to lease a space designed with fire sprinklers versus an un-sprinkled space. There is a hefty price to retrofit sprinklers into an existing space. Smaller distilleries opting for thrift and forgoing sprinklers are confined to the 120 gallons in use, process or storage. Pay careful attention to the process flow for a nano distillery. Managing the process, volumes and quantities of ethanol are crucial to a safe facility that is code-compliant.

There is a legal limit to the amount of alcohol in production.
Once the code is adopted in your jurisdiction, it essentially becomes law. Know which parts of production are regulated by the code: fermentation through the distilling process through. Bottled product does not count as part of the MAQ for your space. Pay close attention to the amount of alcohol in production—between the stripping run and proofing/bottling. Design your process to stay under the 120-gallon limit (or 240 gallons if your space is properly sprinkled) per control area.

Know the properties of ethanol and your process.
Vaporized ethanol is heavier than air. If vaporized ethanol is discharged into the air, it will settle vertically within three feet of the floor and will settle horizontally within 25 feet of the discharge location. Keep anything that provides or uses electricity (i.e., potential ignition sources) outside of that zone. That means power outlets will be 48 inches off the floor. Residential-style refrigerators with their motors in the bottom will be in a different room, or you can opt for a professional model with the motor at the top. Pumps may need to be wall-mounted. Take a hard and critical look at each piece of equipment, how it is powered, where it will be used and at what point in the process, to identify problems preemptively—aka before your still becomes a flamethrower.

Sparks and ethanol vapor don't mix.
There are a number of things that can ignite a fuel-air mixture—heat, static electricity, sparks from hot work (welding/soldering). In a nano distillery, electricity is most likely the potential ignition source. Keep electronics, even low voltage, at least five feet away from potential sources of vapor. Lighting your still—keep light fixtures five feet away from any part of the still. Aging baby barrels—keep the barrels five feet away from any potential source of ignition. Macerating fruit and ethanol—make sure the vessel is five feet away from potential ignition sources.

A cordial is just as flammable as diesel fuel to the Fire Code and OSHA.

Know that anything above 20% ABV—40 proof in the USA—is regulated the same as diesel fuel by the building and fire codes. While there are obvious differences between a water-resistant petroleum product and a water-miscible ethanol product—the codes are written with a very broad brush in this area and are not that specific. Be aware of how the rules are written. When a conflict between the rules and your production plan occur, be flexible and work with your jurisdiction to take a collaborative approach to addressing the issue.

Plastic totes and barrels are not permitted for use with ethanol.

Per NFPA 77 11.1.2.3, "non-conductive portable tanks and IBCs should NOT be used where ignitable ambient vapors are present." In English: Plastic totes and plastic barrels are not permitted for use with ethanol. OSHA also takes issue with storing flammable liquids in "low-melting materials." Use stainless steel.

Chapter Four

Ten Dos and Don'ts
for Working with Your Local Code Officials

Steve Dalbey, Distillery Code Consulting, August 2011
Revised by Ross Topliff, PE - Tops Engineering, PLLC (rosst@topsengineering.com) [January 2017]

Code enforcement is an inexact science. Code officials are human and make mistakes like the rest of us. They are best at those things they do the most, and for many of them that probably doesn't include applying codes to distillery design, buildings or operations. Your attitude and approach to them at the beginning of your project may dictate the level of cooperation you get from them throughout. Clear communications with them about your plans and progress should help to ensure that there are no last-minute requirements dropped in your lap at a time when you expected to be shipping your finished products. The following list of dos and don'ts should help make your interactions with these important officials stay on a positive level.

1. View the code official as a partner, not an enemy. You aren't going to be able to accomplish your goals to design or build and operate your distillery without the help of that person(s). Begin the conversation by expressing your desire to be compliant with code requirements, along with a desire to understand not only what is required but why/how some of those requirements make the process safer. In other words, "I'll do what is required, but help me understand the advantages of following these regulations."

2. Do some research. Find out which fire, building, plumbing and electrical codes (among others) apply to your operation. Most states adopt the international codes, and then some make slight modifications. Find out who the controlling authority is. State officials may defer authority to the local officials, or vice versa. In other words, find out who's in charge and what rules they're charged to enforce. Copies of the code are available online and can usually be found with a quick internet search. (A distiller who has already gone through this in your state can be a huge asset. Check with the ADI for such a person.)

3. Don't take everything you are told to do at face value. Ask questions and, when you're not sure you understand what is being asked of you, ask for code references so you can read them for yourself. No code official should balk at telling you exactly where the requirement can be found. Although the code officials enforce codes for a living, they are still getting most of their information by reading it out of a book or online. You can read, too. The 2015 versions are quite different from the 2012 versions, and many officials are still getting used to them in states that have adopted these. Recommended Fire Protection Practices for Distilled Spirits Beverage Facilities, published by the Distilled Spirits Council of the United States, is an excellent resource, although it is written more for large distilleries.

4. Research and attempt to understand the terminology of flammable liquids, such as "flash point" and "hazard class." The regulations can be confusing, so understanding the basics will go a long way toward preparing you to discuss them intelligently with your local authorities. You may find code alternatives or exceptions that the official missed. Your research and follow-up questions may make the person do more research. If this slows down your design progress, better now than during construction or operation.

5. Work with the code official to develop a full understanding of how the codes apply to your particular situation. If you have a good working relationship with your code officials, you can develop a mutual appreciation for how to apply the codes effectively while enhancing your distilling/blending operations. This may be pie in the sky with some of them, but most do want to work cooperatively while applying the codes properly and effectively.

6. If you are still not clear on what the regulations are saying, ask for assistance from an independent expert. ADI has resources for connecting with those who can assist you, including the author.

7. Attempt to understand the chemical and physical properties of your products. For code-enforcement purposes, alcohol is considered a hazardous material because of its flammability. The properties of alcohol vary significantly based upon the relative amounts of alcohol and water that are present. For instance, a mixture containing less than about 20% alcohol is considered nonflammable and therefore nonhazardous. A good understanding of those differences and their impacts on the code requirements will help you to create a safe environment for your employees, visitors and customers. It will also help you develop

reasonable ways to comply with the letter of the law without doing more than is necessary. Here again, an expert may be invaluable to developing alternatives.

8. Do understand the position the code official is in. The failure to enforce the provisions of a legally adopted code can put that person in legal jeopardy professionally and personally. Asking them to overlook a particular provision of the code simply because it seems a little too much for you may be like asking them to take personal responsibility for something that goes wrong well down the road. A mutual understanding of the codes and the physical/chemical properties of your products will help you to work out reasonable alternatives to the letter of the law that can be documented, protecting the professional interests of all parties.

9. Don't expect the code officials to be able to know and recite all applicable code provisions without a chance to do a little research on their own. Hazardous material codes applicable to distillery operations likely are not something they deal with on a regular basis and may be essentially new. Some of the most important code provisions are contained in the exceptions and alternatives; including some provisions that will benefit you. These can be confusing, so give the official a chance to look these over thoroughly. The background research you do should help bring all of those things out in the open.

10. Do ask if there are any exceptions, alternatives or trade-offs that apply to your situation. Even where no specific exceptions or alternatives exist, there may be some wiggle room where reasonable arguments for alternatives can be considered. Most code officials don't want to be unwavering robots, unable to recognize that a different approach to compliance may actually be more effective in meeting the intent of the codes. This is where a mutual understanding between the code officials and the distillery owners of each other's disciplines and needs can go a long way toward compromise that better serves everyone's interests.

Working cooperatively with your code officials will always bring better results for you. Even if, in the end, you must comply with a requirement that creates a burden for you, knowing its root and purpose should make it easier to swallow. A good understanding of distilling/blending operations by the code official will make it easier for him/her to accept alternatives to the letter of the law.

Scott Sanborn, Sutler's Spirit, Winston-Salem, NC. Photo ©Will Willner, willwillner.com

Chapter Five

Trademark Tips For Small Distillers

Marc Sorini and Bess Morgan

What's in a name? (Or slogan or logo or symbol or other source-identifying device?) Well, turns out a lot. While the craft-spirits industry is a tight-knit and collegial community, businesses must strive to create a unique and distinctive place in the market that makes their products stand out from the rest. For small distillers, who may have leaner advertising budgets than the spirits giants, one effective way to plant your flag in the ground and say, "This is who we are: Come and join us!" is through trademarks.

A trademark is any word, name, symbol, logo and/or device that identifies the goods and services of one party and distinguishes such offerings from those of others.

Below, we provide some tips and recommendations for small distillers to consider when selecting and protecting trademarks.

There's No Benefit in Being Generic: Select Distinctive Marks

One of the most exciting, and often head-scratching, parts of establishing and developing your business is selecting trademarks. Marketing considerations are usually top of mind when selecting trademarks, and rightfully so. Trademarks establish and communicate your business identity. Is your distilling philosophy traditional and sophisticated? Modern and progressive? Off-the-wall and light-hearted? Trademarks reveal your company's personality, and that personality will attract consumers who share, or are attracted to, your point of view.

While marketing considerations are significant when creating brand identity, just as much emphasis should be placed on selecting trademarks that will be considered strong in the eyes of the law. Certain types of trademarks are inherently "strong" and afforded broader legal protections. Other marks are "weak" and afforded less-extensive legal protection or even none at all. The basic trademark categories are:

- **Fanciful**: completely unique and made-up terms with no known meaning other than as a trademark. Examples are Pepsi, Kodak and Xerox. Fanciful marks are considered the strongest type of trademark, meaning they are entitled to a more extensive scope of protection.

- **Arbitrary**: a mark made up of one or more "real" words with a commonly understood meaning, but the words have no relationship to the goods or services with which they are used. Examples are Old Crow whiskey and Apple computers. These marks are also considered strong.

- **Suggestive**: marks that hint at a quality or characteristic of the relevant goods or services, but require some imagination, thought or perception to make the connection. Examples are Chicken of the Sea for tuna and Airbus for airplanes. Suggestive marks are considered weaker than fanciful or arbitrary marks, but can acquire strength over time.

- **Descriptive**: words or phrases that merely describe an ingredient, characteristic, quality, function, feature, purpose or use of the goods or services with which they are used. Examples are: America's Rum, Expertly Distilled, Perfect Vodka. Descriptive marks are only protectable if they have acquired "distinctiveness" or "secondary meaning" to the public through substantially exclusive and continuous use for a considerable amount of time.

- **Generic**: a word that is used to refer to the class or type of goods or services. Examples include vodka, rum, whiskey and tequila. Generic terms are not protectable as trademarks because they must be available for others to use.

Clients often ask whether it is possible to use their surname as, or as part of, a trademark. Generally, if a term is "primarily merely a surname," meaning it does not have a recognized meaning other than as a surname, that name is not protectable as a trademark unless and until it has achieved secondary meaning as an indicator of source for the relevant goods or services. Of course, many surnames do achieve secondary meaning in the eyes of the public, and some very famous trademarks are surnames, including McDonald's, Ford and Wrigley. Owners of well-known name marks may prevent others with the same name from using or registering that name as a trademark. You can imagine you might face a problem with opening a restaurant using any form of the name "McDonald's," even if "McDonald" is your last name. Thus, while it is possible to acquire trademark rights to a brand comprised of a family name, business owners should conduct a clearance search (see next section) to make sure that their name has not already been used and registered by another party in their field of use.

Distillers should also use caution when incorporating geographic terms into their marks. The U.S. Patent and Trademark Office (PTO) will not register a mark that, when used on or in connection with spirits, identifies a geographic place other than the origin of the goods. For example, you should not call your product All-American Vodka if your product is distilled in Canada. Not only does such a name risk disapproval by the PTO, it also puts your ability to obtain a certificate of label approval (COLA) from TTB in jeopardy. And even if you can somehow get such a mark past the PTO and TTB, you still would face the prospect of potential false advertising lawsuits under the federal Lanham Act and state false advertising and unfair competition laws.

Even geographic terms that accurately reflect the origin of your goods will likely be deemed merely descriptive by the PTO, and will not be protectable absent evidence of secondary meaning. Thus, give careful consideration to whether you want to pick a mark that has geographic significance. From a legal perspective, your rights to the mark will be limited, as you cannot prohibit others from using a geographic term to accurately identify the geographic origin of their goods. From a larger business standpoint, consider whether using a geographic indicator may restrict your audience to a particular market. For example, the name Idaho Vodka Co. may not have nationwide or foreign appeal, despite the clever rhyming.

Ultimately, the primary reason to have a trademark is to distinguish your company's offerings from those of a competitor. That is why adopting a distinctive trademark is highly recommended. Others are more likely to use a descriptive trademark without permission, and you will likely have a limited ability to stop others from using your trademark in a purely descriptive manner. So, when selecting trademarks, we recommend coming up with a number of options for consideration, with an emphasis on fanciful, arbitrary or suggestive marks.

Clear Those Marks!

Your team has finally come up with the perfect trademark. You're so excited that you call up legal and yell, "File! File! File!" You're patiently waiting for good news when—cringe—the PTO rejects your application because it finds the same or similar trademark in your field of use, with senior (i.e., prior) rights. You also might receive a demand letter from a senior rights holder demanding you immediately and permanently refrain from any use of, or plans to use, your perfect mark. We write those letters, so we know.

Up-front due diligence could have avoided the foregoing scenarios, or at least an unpleasant surprise. Engaging in trademark clearance is simply part of good industry citizenship. Regardless of whether you are a seasoned distiller or are new to the industry, everyone feels financial pain. And throwing away money and time on a brand you eventually have to abandon cuts deep.

The purpose of trademark clearance is two-fold. First, you avoid infringing prior rights by assessing whether your proposed mark is even available for use. A clearance analysis will compare your proposed mark to those that came before you and assess whether your mark will invite rejection from the PTO and/or objection from third parties. Trademark clearance also can help you determine whether your mark is distinctive. If prior records show you that marks identical or very similar to yours were rejected by the PTO as being merely descriptive or generic, then your application will likely meet a similar fate.

When engaging in trademark clearance, do not limit your clearance searches only to spirits in International Class 33. In analyzing whether a proposed trademark is "confusingly similar" to an existing registration or prior pending application, the PTO has found beer to be "related" to other alcohol beverages – even though the PTO classifies beer separately from other alcohol beverages. In addition, the PTO and the U.S. Court of Appeals for the Federal Circuit (the federal court that hears appeals arising from PTO proceedings) have held alcohol beverages to be "related" to restaurant services in view of evidence that restaurants frequently offer their own private-label wines, and brewpubs are restaurants that offer their own private-label beers. Similar to brewpubs, the restaurant/distillery movement appears to be gaining steam, with restaurants distilling their own spirits and distilleries serving food. Thus, the PTO would likewise have evidence to support a conclusion that spirits and restaurant services are "related" for a likelihood of confusion analysis. Therefore, when clearing your marks, we recommend casting a wide net.

We also recommend expanding your clearance searches beyond marks that are filed or registered with the PTO. As discussed below, in the United States trademark rights are acquired through use. If you come across a website or social media page of a distillery that appears to have started using an identical or similar mark before you, that common-law use can still cause problems for your company even if that senior user has not secured a federal registration.

At a minimum, your clearance searching should include reviewing the PTO's online database and conducting common-law searches using various internet search engines. TTB's online COLA database also provides a valuable tool to identify other alcohol beverages (at least those under TTB's labeling jurisdiction — a category that includes all distilled spirits) sold in interstate commerce that potentially might use the same or a similar mark to the one you wish to use. But we also suggest having a trademark attorney order and review a "comprehensive trademark search report," which provides a more thorough search of the PTO register and includes common-law references such as newspaper articles, magazine articles, internet web pages and business directories. Having a professional search firm research these sources provides a more robust search than you can conduct yourself. While even a comprehensive search cannot provide 100% certainty that a mark is not already in use, it provides some measure of comfort and shows that your company pursued a mark in good faith.

If you're really committed to a trademark despite potential risks identified by the clearance process, you can be proactive about addressing likely conflicts. For example, you can approach a third-party trademark owner and ask that they consent to your use and registration of a mark. You also can explore coexistence with, or offer to purchase, a conflicting mark. Of course, there is no obligation for a senior rights holder to entertain your request, so be prepared to select an alternative mark. For this and other reasons, the decision of whether or not to seek a coexistence arrangement with another trademark owner presents complex issues of business and legal strategy.

As the clearance process can take some time, we recommend giving yourself adequate lead time before you need to commit to a mark and getting legal involved early on in the selection process. That way your advisors can gain a solid understanding of your plans for a brand and can conduct diligence searches effectively.

There are certainly up-front costs associated with trademark clearance, but these costs represent a worthy investment that could help avoid a potential lawsuit or costly re-branding.

Get in the Game—Acquire Rights by Using Your Marks

A common myth is that without a federal trademark registration, you have no rights. In the United States, trademark rights are acquired through use of a mark in commerce, even if the mark is not federally registered. The moment you sell your spirits, marked with your trademark, to a customer or transport your trademarked goods to distributors or retailers, you are acquiring common-law trademark rights. These common-law rights may permit you to successfully challenge a third party from later attempting to use and/or register a mark identical or highly similar to yours.

Common-law rights do have limitations. They extend to the geographic area of actual use and a reasonable surrounding area. For example, if you have only used your mark in and around the Detroit metropolitan area, chances are slim that you will be able to successfully prevent someone from using a mark identical or highly similar to yours in Texas.

For this and other reasons, there are clear benefits to federal registration. One of the chief benefits of federal registration is that it sets a constructive first-use date based on the filing date of your application, which gives you nationwide priority over others who are using or attempting to register the same or similar mark after that point in time. In other words, with a federal registration your trademark rights become national as of your constructive use date, as opposed to your common-law rights that are dependent on your geographic areas of actual use. Bear in mind, however, that a party whose common-law rights are senior to yours still has the right to use their trademark within their geographic area of use, notwithstanding your federal registration. A savvy common-law rights holder might require that you exclude from your trademark registration their market area or negotiate some form of coexistence.

Provided your mark has passed the clearance process, it is in your best interest to begin using your trademark in U.S. commerce to start establishing your common-law rights while you consider, and ideally pursue, federal registration.

Get Creative

Not only word marks enjoy trademark protection. To build a robust trademark portfolio, also consider protecting logos and designs, which may consist of a symbol (e.g., the Bacardí bat), a combination of words and designs or words presented in a stylized font (e.g., Absolut in its signature block lettering). Slogans and taglines also are protectable designations of source, for example, "It's Miller Time," "Just Do It," "Taste the Rainbow" and "The Happiest Place on Earth."

Spirits trademarks can consist of various elements on a bottle label, including the name of the product, name of the distillery, logos and design elements (e.g., a shield or crest, decorative banners, a background pattern). They might also include the combination of all of those elements and how they are presented on the label or configured on the bottle. You can also explore protecting the shape or color of your bottle if it is unique and does not serve a functional purpose.

Trademarks come in many forms. Being aware of, and obtaining protection for, the various trademarkable elements of your business will increase your company's valuable intellectual property assets and put you in a stronger position to enforce your marks against unauthorized third-party users.

Conclusion

The growing number of small distillers highlights the desirability of joining a collegial and creative industry. By understanding some basics about trademark selection and protection, you can build your business upon a solid foundation and focus on expanding your empire rather than defending against attacks.

Marc Sorini is a partner in the law firm of McDermott Will & Emery LLP, based in the firm's Washington, D.C. office. He is the leader of the firm's Alcohol Regulatory & Distribution Group. Recognized as one of the leading lawyers in his field by Best Lawyers and the Chambers USA directory, he advises breweries, distilleries, wineries and importers on regulatory, litigation, licensing, distribution, advertising product formulation and taxation issues.

Bess Morgan is an associate in the law firm of McDermott Will & Emery LLP and is based in the firm's Los Angeles office. She focuses her practice on trademark prosecution, counseling, licensing and dispute matters. Bess advises clients on the selection and adoption of new trademarks, renders opinions on the availability and proper use of trademarks and assists in the enforcement and protection of clients' trademark portfolios. Bess also advises clients on a variety of other intellectual property transactional matters including: copyright and right of publicity clearance, protection and licensing; contests, sweepstakes and raffles; recovery of domain names through UDRP actions; licensing and distribution agreements; compliance with advertising and marketing regulations; and IP due diligence and counseling in connection with corporate transactions such as mergers and acquisitions.

[This article first appeared in the Spring 2016 edition of *Artisan Spirits* magazine.]

Lost Ark Distilling Company, Columbia, MD

Chapter Six

Correct Alcohol Dilution Calculation for Distillers

Gary Spedding, Brewing and Distilling Analytical Services, LLC

Distillers are often required to make dilutions to lower the alcohol strength of their products. While many solutions can simply be mixed in appropriate volumes to yield the desired ending concentration, this is not the case for alcohol and water mixtures; when alcohol and water are mixed together, molecular interactions and spatial reconfiguration (space-filling) leads to a contraction effect which impacts the total final volume. This is sometimes also known as the excess volumes of mixing, and this effect can cause problems related to obtaining the correct final amount of alcohol in the diluted spirit. Furthermore, this is not a fixed volume reduction but varies across the spectrum of alcohol concentration.

Most distillers use the tried-and-true Tax and Trade Bureau Gauging Manual method when reducing cask-strength alcohol to bottling strength (based on determinations at 60° F). While this is an appropriate method, it can be tedious and is not the only one available to assist in correcting alcohol volume dilutions. Here, with an example and a caveat, is an alternate method (based on 20° C determinations). The caveat being that this works well with traditional high alcohol, though low extract strength (traditional) spirits. Highly sweetened and flavored products are not ideally suited to this or even the Gauging Manual method.

Alcohol dilution calculations

The method outlined here requires the use of legal metrology tables, known as the OIML tables, which can be consulted for alcohol-water solution density values and the corresponding alcohol values. These tables are available online: (https://www.oiml.org/en/files/pdf_r/r022-e75.pdf/view). Table Va refers to density and alcohol by weight (ABW) values, and Table Vb refers to density vs. alcohol by volume (ABV); table Vb is the one used here.

Calculating the amount of water needed to dilute a given volume of alcohol to a lower percentage

While there are several applications on this overall approach, an important one is in the use for the dilution of matured spirits to bottling strength (proofing).

Again, it is to be noted that for modern formulations, the density of the sample might be reflective of not only the original alcohol-water mix but also sugars and flavorings used. So, the actual specific gravity of the sample might become important here. The usual proofing rules on obscuration solids if between 400–600 mg/100 mL will not interfere as much on these calculations, as there is still essentially a hydro-alcoholic mixture at play (the multitude of congeners adding only a fractional amount to the density). Consulting the TTB website for the proof obscuration method and regulations and being aware of the composition of the specific products under consideration will be important when using the approach outlined here. [TTB gauging procedures and proofing/proof obscuration details here: http://www.ttb.gov/foia/gauging_manual_toc.shtml#27:1.0.1.1.25.4.504.1]

Other types of tables exist which show the amount of water to add to a given volume of alcohol of specific concentration to obtain a desired final lower alcohol concentration; these tables may be found in the literature but are often limited in scope. Alternatively, an equation can be applied, which acts independently of the final volume of the hydro-alcoholic solution desired, to yield the appropriate parameters specific to each required dilution operation. It involves a simple algebraic resolution, introduced here:

$$\%_{v/v\ conc} \times V_{conc} = \%_{v/v\ dilute} \times xV_{dilute} \qquad [1]$$

Where v/vconc and v/vdilute represent the initial and desired final percentage alcohol by volume concentrations, and Vconc and Vdilute the volumes of the concentrated and final diluted alcohol solutions respectively. From Equation 1, a formula can be derived that allows for the determination of the final volume of a hydro-alcoholic solution which undergoes the volumetric contraction discussed above:

$$xV_{dilute} = \frac{\%v/v\ conc}{\%v/v\ dilute} \times V_{conc} \qquad [2]$$

Example (volumes in milliliters):

$$xV_{dilute} = \frac{95\%}{40\%} \times 100mL = 237.5mL$$

This value is important in cross-checking the final alcohol concentration following mixing of the defined volumes of alcohol and water. Now, multiplying the volume by its density (obtained from OIML Table Vb) leads to the final weight of the diluted solution, and then the water of dilution to be added is determined:

$$water\ to\ be\ added\ = y_{water} = xV_{dilute} \times \rho_{dilute} - V_{conc} \times \rho_{conc} \qquad [\mathbf{3}]$$

Where y = volume of water to add and = the respective densities of the concentrated alcohol solution and the final diluted sample. Again, the OIML table Vb can be referenced for these density values. For this example, plugging in the numbers gives 144 mL water to add to 100 mL 95% alcohol by volume solution to yield 244 mL final solution. [Note: Here the volume contraction is 244 – 237.5 = 6.5 mL or 2.66%. This significant contraction is now corrected for in making this mix of alcohol and water—and voilà! There is an accurately made sample of known alcohol strength!]

While the above equation (Equation 3) is all that would be needed in most cases, a more extended explanation is now presented for the sake of completeness and to show the steps required in more detail. Equation 3 can be rewritten:

$$y_{water} = \frac{\%v/v\ conc}{\%v/v\ dilute} \times V_{conc} \times \rho_{dilute} - V_{conc} \times \rho_{conc} \qquad [\mathbf{4}]$$

Then the volume of the concentrated alcohol can be set as 100 parts; from this point, it is easy to determine the volume units of water to add.

$$y_{water} = 100 \times \frac{\%v/v\ conc \times \rho_{dilute} - \%v/v\ conc \times \rho_{conc}}{\%v/v\ dilute} \qquad [\mathbf{5}]$$

Or by further simplifying Equation 5, the variant Equation 6 can be used:

$$y_{water} = 100 \times \frac{\%v/v\ conc \times \rho_{dilute}}{\%v/v\ dilute} - \rho_{conc} \qquad [\mathbf{6}]$$

Plugging the requisite values into the variant equations (5 or 6) again leads to 144 units (mL, liters, 100 liters, gallons, etc.) of water to be added to 100 units of 95% alcohol. The use of such equations and the OIML tables will assist in defining precise dilutions for the distiller. The reader may like to try the approach (using the OIML tables) to show how to reduce a 50% ABV (100 proof) barrel-strength spirit to 40% (80 proof) bottling strength. The answer should show that 25.5 (rounded) units of pure mineral-free water should be added to 100 units of the 50% ABV barrel-strength spirit. In practice, for any dilution operation, the final alcohol content should of course be tested to be certain of the outcome.

[Footnote: Regarding the equations and OIML tables, it is to be noted that these are based on 20° C evaluations. In the USA, proof refers to two times the alcohol by volume (ABV) percentage as determined at 60° F (15.56° C). There is only a slight difference in the alcohol by volume values at 60° F vs. 20° C, but readers should be aware of this when making process adjustments in their facilities.]

A wooden mill

Beehive Distilling in South Salt Lake, UT

Chapter Seven

Nano Distillery Record Keeping

Donald Snyder, President, Whiskey Systems Online
www.whiskeysystems.com

One of the biggest challenges that nano distilleries must overcome is staying in full compliance with the Tax and Trade Bureau (TTB) regulations. Small craft distilleries are under the same regulations and scrutiny as the largest distilleries in the country. The distilleries shipping millions of cases per year must complete the same monthly reports and maintain the same daily logs as the nano distilleries shipping one hundred cases per year. The largest distilleries employ dozens of full-time government compliance staff and bookkeepers to ensure every report and excise tax return is accurate and auditable. Unfortunately for most small craft distilleries, monthly reporting and compliance often falls in priority behind running the business, maintaining inventory, developing new brands, shipping orders, managing the tasting room and all the other day-to-day pressures.

What Is the TTB Looking For?

The TTB wants visibility into the complete life cycle of your distilled spirits, from the amount of grains used to how much spirit came off the still to how many bottles were filled to how many cases were removed from the distillery. The TTB needs to see losses at each step of the operation, including "angel's share" evaporation loss, bottling run loss and any spirits that were destroyed. Records of all these daily transactions are the critical support documentation the distillery must keep to file its monthly operations reports and maintain in the event of an audit. The TTB wants a clear and transparent picture of what happens to every "proof gallon" of alcohol in your distillery.

What Is a Proof Gallon?

The TTB requires that everything be reported in "proof gallons" (PG), which is a universal way to express how much alcohol is in a tank, barrel or bottle, taking into consideration its proof and percent alcohol by volume (ABV). A "wine gallon" (WG) is the basic volumetric measure of the number of liquid gallons in a vessel. For example, a 50-gallon tank filled with a distilled spirit would have

50 WG, regardless of its proof. However, if the tank were filled with 50 gallons of 190-proof (95% ABV) vodka, it would have a lot more taxable alcohol than if it were filled with 50 gallons of 40-proof (20% ABV) liqueur. Because distilled spirits are taxed by the proof gallon, just knowing the number of gallons (or WG) is not enough to calculate the excise taxes owed. The current standard excise tax rate distilleries pay is $2.70[1] per proof gallon. The equation to calculate the proof gallons and tax liability in a vessel is:

Wine Gallons x (Proof/100) = Proof Gallons x $13.50/PG = $ Excise Tax Liability

> *Vodka example:*
>
> 50 Wine Gallons x (190 Proof/100) = 95 Proof Gallons x $2.70/PG = $256.50 Excise Tax due if bottled and removed from the distillery

> *Liqueur example:*
>
> 50 Wine Gallons x (40 Proof/100) = 20 Proof Gallons x $2.70/PG = $54 Excise Tax due if bottled and removed from the distillery.

What Is Expected of a Nano Distillery Each Month?

As soon as a distillery obtains its federal permit (DSP), it is immediately required to file three reports each month: production, storage and processing. Even if a distillery doesn't do anything during a month, it is required to file these three reports filled in with zeros. The operations reports are due by the 14th of the following month. Failure to complete these reports on time and correctly can be met with steep penalties.

The production report is a summary of what went into the still and what came out of the condenser. This report aggregates all the fermentable materials used in the month (e.g., gallons of molasses, pounds of grains, etc.), how many proof gallons of spirits were redistilled and how many proof gallons of each spirit type were distilled and where the gallons went. The report breaks down the different types of alcohol into columns, including whiskey, vodka, rum, gin, etc. Every proof gallon of good, drinkable alcohol that came off the still must be accounted for whether it went into a barrel, into a tank, directly to processing for bottling or even transferred out to another distillery.

---

1   The standard tax rate (as of press time) distilleries pay is $2.70 per proof gallon on the first 100,000 proof gallons removed or imported, and $13.34 per proof gallon on the next 22.13 million proof gallons removed or imported. Since a nano distilleries, by definition, produce less than 10,000 proof gallons a year, they will use the $2.70 rate. Because the Craft Beverage Modernization and Tax Reform Act of 2017 is set to expire at the end of 2019, unless legislation is passed, the rate will increase to $13.50 a proof gallon on all distilled spirits in the year 2020.

The storage report is an ongoing balance of all the spirits in storage tanks and barrels. The report includes what was in inventory at the start of the month, what was received (including what was transferred in from another distillery), what was sent to processing for bottling, what was lost or destroyed and what was left in inventory at the end of the month.

The processing report is like the storage report, as it is an ongoing report of inventory balances each month. This report is broken down into two parts: bulk ingredients and finished goods. On this report, distilleries show how many proof gallons were bottled and how many proof gallons of finished cases were withdrawn from bond that month.

Federal Excise Tax Returns

The final report every distiller (big or small) must complete is the most important: the federal excise tax return. A distillery that pays less than $50,000 in excise tax in one calendar year can pay excise tax returns each quarter. A distillery that pays more than $50,000 in one calendar year must pay excise taxes every 15 days. Federal excise taxes are owed only after a full case is withdrawn from the distillery's bonded space. For example, taxes are owed on a case of bottles the date it is removed from the distillery's bonded space and brought over to the gift shop or tasting room or shipped to a distributor. Keep a meticulous record of every case withdrawn from the distillery and pay the taxes for every case removed during the tax period.

If a distiller is overwhelmed by all the regulations and reporting requirements, there is no need to reinvent the compliance wheel. Instead of spending hours developing an internal spreadsheet, seek out craft-distillery-focused software like Whiskey Systems Online to help streamline and automate the monthly TTB reporting and compliance. A secure, cloud-based system can ensure that distilleries stay up-to-date on all regulations, ensure that all the required daily logs are available and help the distiller be confident in the event of an on-site audit.

Brennerei Lüthy

New Harbor Distillery, South Africa

Chapter Eight

Essential Equipment for a Startup Nano Distillery

Brad Plummer, Farallon Gin Works, San Carlos, CA

Building a craft nano distillery from scratch is a complex undertaking, and no one will be holding your hand as you burn through your capital. (Most people keep their day job.) It can take months to get a building permit for your location, and then it requires a labyrinth of paperwork to obtain federal, state and local regulatory licenses. And the fire department permit for a distillery can be the most difficult permit to obtain. (You have been warned.)

On top of these challenges, it can take a considerable amount of time just to source the equipment. That is what this chapter addresses.

The following list of items comprises what most people need to purchase to open a nano distillery, although some of the items will vary depending on your chosen production process and the products you make. (You won't need a brewhouse if you partner with a local brewery.) Depending on your resourcefulness and determination, all of the items listed can be had for under $100,000 (not including the build-out and rent on the building, of course). Many of the items listed below can be sourced on Google and eBay. Google will not, however, give you a complete list of, for example, distilling equipment manufacturers, roller mill companies or cooperages. Many of these specialty items can be sourced through ADI's *Distillers' Resource Directory*, which you can obtain by joining ADI (www.distilling.com).

• Office computer system, $1,500+

> You need an internet connection, a desktop or laptop, and a printer. Also purchase a dock for streaming music, and a fridge. A good coffee maker is a must.

> To run a distillery, you will be required to keep monthly TTB records of the distilling process and to pay monthly excise taxes. Many state regulatory agencies allow only online access to their licensing systems (i.e., paper submissions are not accepted). Use your computer to create

a logbook and write down everything from mashing to distilling run. It is recommended that documentation follows every mash through fermentation, distillation and bottling. Attaching clipboards or plastic sleeves to every tank can be helpful. You can try a distillery-focused software like Whiskey Systems Online to track your production and inventory. TTB may want to see these records.

• Nano still, $600–$25,000

For $600 you can buy an 8-gallon "milk can" still, with a two-inch dual-purpose tower with a controller. Consider it at best a starter or pilot still.

If you shop around, it's possible to find a 53-gallon still with immersion heating elements and an electric variable controller for $5,000 to $7,000. You can also find a copper 100-gallon direct-fire (gas) still for less than $20,000. If, however, you want to make corn whiskey, you will have to expand your shopping list to include a roller mill, a corn cooker and a steam boiler. (You can use an electric boiler.) The cost of the boiler and piping (installed by a union pipe fitter) will cost more than the still. With a steam boiler you might need city "use" permits, and in some cases, a state permit to operate—check your local and state codes. All these items to make corn whiskey quickly add up and can break your budget. (Electric systems are cheaper.)

If, however, you want to make single-malt whiskey, you can get started by buying wort or beer wash from a local microbrewery, or build or buy a mash tun. (Mashing barley is simple when compared to cooking corn.)

Distilling vodka on a nano scale requires having a vodka head with plates (more $$$). Many distillers purchase a still with two heads. This allows you to switch out the head and make whiskey or vodka. This type of distilling unit can also be easily expanded. Buying four or five of them can give you the capacity to run 100+ gallons of wash to create 10 gallons of spirits.

The drawback of an electric immersion element still is that you can't easily run fruit. It's necessary to have an agitator running during distillation to keep the electric elements in the still from scorching your product. Another way to avoid scorching is to buy a bain-marie (double boiler) still. With it, you can distill fruit or whiskey on the grain.

Buy books, watch YouTube videos and use Google to its fullest, as the internet holds heaps of information. A full list of large and small distilling equipment can be found on www.distilling.com.

Join a discussion group at www.ADIForums.com and ask other potential distillers about distilling equipment. The forum is open (free) to all, so ask any questions about distilling and someone will respond.

Listed below are just a handful of the dozens of companies that manufacture distilling equipment. Choose carefully, as most of the equipment is made in China. Know what you're buying. Use your library, tap the internet. And join www.ADIforums.com: It's free.

www.distillery-equipment.com
www.milehidistilling.com
www.hillbillystills.com
www.stilldragon.com
www.hogastills.com

• Brewing and Fermentation Equipment (Optional)

    Many nano distilleries will begin their operations using alcohol (NGS) purchased from a third party, rather than brew and ferment their own. This is especially true for distillers interested in making gin and other clear spirits. However if you plan to make whiskey etc. from scratch, unless you partner with a microbrewery to make your wash, you will have to purchase brewing and fermentation equipment.

    If you are using a still with internal elements and want to brew with grain, you will have to separate the grain from the wash before you distill to avoid scorching the plant material, which will ruin the batch. A variety of online suppliers sell smaller-scale brewing equipment (mash tun, lauter tun, fermenters, chillers, etc.). The most expensive of these will be the mash/lauter tun, used for cooking the grain into wash and then separating out the spent grains. For a pure corn wash you will need a corn cooker, and for rum you will need a mash vessel suited for handling molasses. An empty IBC tote makes an effective yet inexpensive fermenter.

    A full discussion on the equipment needed to brew and ferment is beyond the scope of this book. Many DIY solutions can be found, which will cut costs dramatically. But expect to spend at least as much as you do on your still for a full brewhouse setup. Check the ADI Forum for used equipment, and the ADI *Distillers' Resource Directory* for an exhaustive list of trusted equipment suppliers.

• Bench still, $600

    A small tabletop still (0.5–2 L) is necessary for experimenting with new recipes and for obscuration/assay runs to determine the alcohol content of spirits with suspended solids or dissolved sugars (e.g., liqueurs).
        http://www.heartmagic.com/EssentialDistiller.html
        http://adamschittenden.com/

• Stainless steel collection vessel, $100+

    The 50-liter (13-gal.) fusti tanks are a must, as they are easy to drag around. (Buy 10 of them.) You can also blend in the 100/200/500-liter tanks.
    http://www.napafermentation.com/fusti-cans1.html
    https://www.uline.com/BL_8187/Stainless-Steel-Drums

- Pallet jack, $300

    For moving bags of grain, cases of bottles and barrels of alcohol.

    www.Grainger.com

    www.NorthernTool.com

    www.Uline.com

- Electric pump (cart-mounted), $600

    Good for filtration cycles of final product (low-proof) or moving product around. Not for use with high-proof alcohol. Invest in a good, variable-speed pump with a remote controller for those times when you're alone or up on a ladder, pumping out a tank.

    http://www.gwkent.com

- Pneumatic pump, $400–$2,000+

    Spark-free, fire-safe power for transferring high-proof (flammable) spirit.

    $400 (nylon housing, ½-inch ports, 7 gallons per minute [gpm]) to $3,500 (steel housing, 2-inch ports, 200 gpm). Many distillers use gravity to drain tanks into drums. You can also use a forklift to lift a tote and drain its contents into a steel drum.

    http://www.gwkent.com/

- Air compressor, $300–$500

    For operating pneumatic pumps. 30–60+ gallon reservoir for small pumps. (A smaller reservoir is OK if the compressor is rated for continuous operation.) Check local hardware stores. You can also find these used. Look into buying a used dental compressor; they are oil-free. Make sure to install an in-line drying filter to ensure that you have no moisture coming out of your compressor.

    www.grainger.com

    www.northerntool.com

- Storage tanks (plastic & steel) $600–$800; used under $300

    Used food-grade plastic drums with removable tops are available for blending and short-term storage ($20–$40, check Craigslist in your area). For longer-term storage, stainless steel tanks are required. Steel tanks can also be leased for $1.50 per day. The 270-gallon plastic totes are great for storage. Ethanol cannot be stored in a vessel over 125 gallons without a UL listing.

    http://www.gwkent.com/

http://www.hooversolutions.com/
http://custom-metalcraft.com/

- Stainless steel work tables, $200–$500 from restaurant supply stores
    Welded tables are sturdier but more expensive. Bolt-together tables
    should suffice for most applications.

- Reverse osmosis water filtration system, $300+
    Most small operations can get by with a 300-gallon-per-day (GPD) sys-
    tem, depending on operations. Larger industrial systems can be leased.
    http://www.premierwatersystems.net/

- Heavy-duty floor scale, ~$500–$1,500
    Many distilleries use weight to proof alcohol for bottling. The weighing
    surface should be 48" square for pallets, 24" for drums. Digital, certified
    legal for trade (NTEP), rated for 2,000 to 5,000 lbs. (48") or 1,000 lbs.
    (24"). For more information regarding scale requirements (including
    incrementation and calibration) and usage regulations, refer to 27 CFR
    Sec. 19.181-185.
    http://www.scaledepot.com/industrial-scales/drum-scales/

- Bottle filler, $500–$1,700
    Most distillers use wine fillers (with 4–6 nozzles) that are gravity-fed.
    You can fill 200 bottles per hour with an Enolmatic filler (about $400),
    which has a vacuum pump, making it easier to deal with than gravi-
    ty-fed systems. It also has an option for in-line filtering so you can filter
    as you bottle.
    http://www.gwkent.com/
    http://morewinemaking.com/

- Label printer, $2,500 for printer, $150 for set of ink cartridges
    On-demand digital label printers can be used with custom die-cut label
    stock or with off-the-shelf label shapes (cheaper). This can be a cost-ef-
    fective means of producing labels in small runs. Label stock varies
    according to size and count.

    To save money, go with printed labels at a cost of 25–50 cents each.
    Labels can be applied by hand until you hit 1,000 cases. (Pro tip: Design
    a one-piece label rather than separate front and back labels. You'll be
    saving hours of labeling time.) Silk-screen labels are another option,

but you need to commit to several pallets of bottles.
https://www.primeralabel.com/
www.dispensamatic.com
www.smythco.com

• Labeling machine, $1,500+
Electric and manual machines are available.

Do budget money and buy a labeling machine, as labeling by hand
is very, very, time consuming. Many distilleries have bottling parties
to help out. (Note: Most labelers only work with round bottles, and
tapered bottles require taper-specific machine designs, which are
more expensive.)
http://www.racelabel.com/
https://easylabeler.com/
www.impactprintsolutions.com

• Hoses and fittings, $75–$150
Hoses (1- to 3-inch diameter with tri-clamp fittings). Bulk hose is the
most economical. (Fitted with tri-clamp barb inserts after being cut
to size.) ~$3-$4 per foot. 1-inch Goodyear Nutriflo hose, $3.50 per foot,
high-proof alcohol safe, heat safe.

• Clamps & fittings (tri-clamps, gaskets + extras).
Tri-clamp barb inserts (x 2 per hose), silicone gaskets, tri-clamps, hose
clamps. Also make sure to purchase butterfly valves, (e.g., 1.5-inch)
~$80 each.
http://www.gwkent.com/

• Flowmeter, $800+
For measuring liquids during transfer.
http://www.gwkent.com/econo-turbine-flow-meter-1in-1.html
www.gpimeter.net

• Stainless steel racking canes, $70
For pumping liquids out of/into drums or barrels. With tri-clamp fittings.
http://www.gwkent.com/

• Nozzle for filling barrels, $150–$300
Purpose-built or form-fitting components (butterfly valve + elbow).

http://www.gwkent.com/barrel-filler-1-1-2-tc.html

- Cleaners (citric acid, PBW), $75
    https://amzn.com/B001D6IVZG
    https://morewinepro.com/
    http://www.fivestarchemicals.com/breweries/craft-brewers/
    products/

- Mixing paddles, $40
    Boat oars may be tempting but will eventually absorb liquids, and
    varnish can flake off. Stainless steel is preferred, available from local
    restaurant supply stores.
    https://www.unionjackstable.com/

- Thermometers, $150
    Certified, calibrated glass thermometer, required by TTB.
    http://www.labdepotinc.com/

- Hydrometers, $250+
    Certified, calibrated precision high-proof alcohol hydrometers (0–200
    proof, 70–90 proof, 140–160 proof) are required for proofing prod-
    uct. Buy several cheap 0–200 proof hydrometers for day-to-day work
    because you will be breaking them. Keep your certified hydrometers for
    proofing in a hydrometer rack in a safe place.
    http://www.labdepotinc.com/
    http://www.gwkent.com/

- Digital alcohol meter, $2,500
    A digital meter is a must (budget for it) as it's a time-saver. Although
    not allowed by TTB for bringing product to final bottling strength, it
    works well for routine in-house measurements or to get your product
    close enough to then use the precision glass hydrometers.
    www.anton-paar.com/us-en/
    www.mt.com (density meter)
    www.rudolphresearch.com

- Filtration system: housings from $500–$700, cartridges from $50–$100
    Common housings include cartridge (10- or 20-inch) and lenticular, or
    plate-and-frame. Useful retention sizes include rough strainer "sock,"
    100 micron, 10 micron, 1 micron and smaller. (Anything below 0.8

Anton Paar Alcohol Meter

Fast. Accurate. Reliable. These are not words commonly used to describe checking spirit proof when doing your cuts during a spirit run or finishing proof before bottling.

Before the Anton Paar digital hydrometer, we used a simplistic glass hydrometer to measure the proof of all distilled spirits produced at our distillery, both as a quick spirit-proof check at the still (think parrot) and then before bottling to cut down to official proof with our big, clunky IRS-certified hydrometer.

We all know the routine. You fill a glass beaker with the distilled spirit. Place the glass hydrometer in that fluid, and take an eyeball reading of where the glass hydrometer shows the proof level to be at the surface of the fluid. Then we would need to take a temperature reading using a NIST-certified thermometer to check the temperature of the distilled solution and read a chart that says what the "actual" proof is after temperature compensation is considered. This was extremely time-consuming and had the potential (likely) for possible errors to take place. The amount of time to set this up was about five minutes per reading, and we do it dozens of time per day.

We were fortunate enough to get our hands on an Anton Paar digital handheld hydrometer and, man, what a difference this thing makes.

Now we are able to simply place the sampling tube into the distilled solution, press the sampling plunger, and the Anton Paar takes the reading of the alcohol percentage of the solution and does all the temperature compensation for us, giving an accurate and reliable reading in a matter of seconds. Yes, seconds. Yes, accurate. Yes, reliable. I actual said those things when talking about spirit-proof reading.

In addition to this, we now find ourselves checking spirit-run proof more frequently throughout the day because of the ease of use with the Anton Paar, which in turn makes us more consistent with our cuts, reducing the flavor profile variability of batch-to-batch finished product. We all want consistent product from batch to batch.

Though the Anton Paar model we use (model DMA 35) is not TTB-certified, we use it to get as close to fin-

ished bottling proof as possible, then bring out our semi-trusty certified glass hydrometer to finish the proofing (still saving much time).

Look, I know these digital hydrometers are not cheap. I resisted buying one because of the cost, but after doing some simple math, I have paid for this thing in time savings after only three months of use. The stress relief is also worth the money alone.

So, go out and get one. I promise you won't regret it. Ask anyone who uses one of these and they will tell you the same.

Sean Smiley, Owner, Head Distiller, State 38 Distilling, Golden, CO

microns will start to remove flavor and color.) Chill unit may be used for whiskey and spirits fermented from grain.

> http://www.gwkent.com/
> http://www.scottlaboratories.com/
> http://www.pall.com/
> http://www.allfilters.com/

• Fire extinguishers, $150–$500

> Handheld, in addition to fire-suppression systems (e.g., sprinklers). Should be rated ABC. Check local fire code for number and placement. Purchase reconditioned from local fire safety equipment supplier.

• Laboratory items and glassware, $250–$400

> Graduated cylinders (1 L, 500 mL, 100 mL), Ehrlenmeyer flasks (1 L, 500 mL), portable pH meter, lab scale (0-200 grams), safety goggles, a respirator and protective rubber gloves.
>
> www.labdepotinc.com
> www.veegee.com

• Glass carboys, 3 and 5 or 6 gallons, $25+

> Use only for mixing, blending or recipe development, etc., not for distillate collection. (Note: They are hard to clean compared to the Italian fustis cans.)
>
> http://morewinemaking.com/

• IBC totes, $80–$150 (used)

> Useful for storing water or spirit, or as economy mashing/fermenting vessels. Check local Craigslist for used totes. Be certain that used totes previously contained only food products. (Totes are also included with purchase of bulk NGS and when empty can be repurposed as fermenters.)

• Wet/dry vacuum, $80–$100

> Home Depot or your local hardware store

• Work carts and two-wheel dolly, $50+

> Home Depot, Lowe's or a local hardware store

• Chest freezer, $200+

With refrigerator mode (to keep beer).
Best Buy

• Fruit press, $350+

Distillers often focus on those shiny copper stills and neglect the whole mashing and fermentation side of the process. If you plan to distill fruit or grapes, you will need a good crusher and press. (Alternatively, you can buy the juice, but it can be pricy.)

When fermenting fruit, use a tank that is jacketed and run cold water through the jacket to maintain the fermentation temperature. This will save you from buying a glycol system. Alternately, an immersion chiller can be made from a copper coil and used to keep the fermentation cool.
http://amazon.com
http://morewinemaking.com/

• Pressure washer, $100–$200

Great for cleaning tanks. Should be at least 1,500 psi. Can be found at Home Depot and local hardware stores.

• Sampling jars, $5

For recipe development and product testing. Canning jars are perfect, 0.5- to 2-L size.
www.Freundcontainer.com

• Botanical steeping bags, $25

Grain socks for brewing work nicely.
www.morewinemaking.com
www.midwestsupplies.com
www.mcmaster.com

• 5-gallon buckets w/lids, $5 each

Home Depot, Uline or Grainger. Make sure the plastic is food grade.

• Forklift or walk-behind hydraulic lift, $1,000–$5, 000 (used on eBay) or new for $12K–$15K
A late model, low-hour Toyota or Hyster are the most reliable

• Oak barrels (5, 8, 10, 15, 20, 23, 30, and 53 gal.), $100–$600

Required if you are aging or resting spirits in wood. Reconditioned barrels can be purchased at www.kelvincooperage.com and www.recoopbarrels.com. A full list of U.S. and European cooperages can be found at:
www.distilling.com.
www.blackswanbarrels.com
www.thebarrelmill.com

• Industrial shelf racks (pallet-size) and barrel racks, $1,200

10' x 25' section. Maximize floor space by stacking pallets and totes. They can be purchased used. Check local service listings for "freight-handling systems." Metal barrel racks are useful because they can be moved and stacked. Again, check eBay for racks or barrel racks.
http://www.rackandmaintenance.com/
www.Westernsquare.com

• Magnetic stir plate, $70–$100

For yeast propagation. Can be built DIY or purchased online from a laboratory supply company.
http://www.labdepotinc.com/
www.veegee.com
www.cynmar.com

• Grain mill, $1,500+

Used mills are available.

To make corn whiskey, a hammer mill is best for turning corn, wheat and rye into a fine powder for cooking mash.

To make single-malt whiskey wash, use a mash tun with a false bottom. Buy a roller mill and crack your barley at 1/32". Use a single-step mash infusion and produce wort for fermentation. (A two-hour barley mashing process is simple compared to the six hours it takes to heat, cook and cool a corn wash.)
www.coloradomillequipment.com
www.k-malt.com

• Neutral grain spirit (NGS) supplier: 55 gal. @ 190 proof, around $700

Numerous companies supply high-quality, bulk high-poof sprits. You can also buy organic bulk whiskey, rum and gins. Some can be found organic. Many nano (gin) distillers buy bulk spirits, water it down to

100 proof and then redistill it to remove heads. This method of making gin is especially common in Europe. For a full listing of NGS producers, go to www.distilling.com

• Compliance resources

Applying for a Distilled Spirits Plant (DSP) application with the TTB can be a long and painful process. Budget at least five months between starting the application and receiving a final approval from the TTB. Every owner who has more than 10% equity ownership in the distillery must submit an Owner Officer Information (OOI) application, which is a very intrusive background check. After all owners have submitted their OOI applications, the distiller can submit an application for a DSP. This is traditionally done online at ttb.gov. There are many resources available to help with your application, including alcohol-focused law groups like Bevlaw.com and online resources like Whiskey Systems Online's New Business Development tools.

www.ttb.gov/faqs/
www.cas-cas-compliance.com
www.whiskeyresources.com

• A patient, supportive partner. Priceless.

• A day job. Keep yours as long as possible.

Steam Boiler

The expense of buying and installing a boiler to get a nano distillery up and running can be a real headache for people on a tight budget. Purchase and installation of a steam boiler for a small (50- to 150-gallon) nano still and corn cooker will be one of the most expensive items in your distillery. At the low end, a boiler can cost $5,000 and installation $15,000. This is why most nano stills are powered using electric elements or direct fire.

Talk to a boiler specialist to calculate the BTUs necessary to power your corn cooker and still. Most still manufacturers will tell you the BTUs necessary to run the still and recommend a steam boiler company in your area.

Installing a boiler will on average cost twice what you estimate and can easily cost more than the boiler. Electric steam boilers are usually less expensive than gas-fired boilers, but require huge amounts of electricity. Talk to the city planning department and local fire department about permitting requirements. Some states and cities do not require permits for boilers below a certain size or power rating. For those that do, most have never seen a distillery and will take their time making a ruling. Many cities require that a gas-fired steam boiler be in a separate room, although rural fire departments may not require this. You never know what they will require you to install, but expect it to cost time and money. It is their job to protect the public, and boiler installation and operation is their territory.

John Reid, Owner/Distiller, Old Flatbed Distillery
Meridian, ID
oldflatbeddistillery@yahoo.com

Part Three
Production Techniques

Chapter Nine

How Distillation Works

Distillation is a physical process in which compounds are separated by virtue of their different boiling points and vapor pressures.

The separation in distillation occurs when a mixture of compounds in the still is brought to boil. As a simplification, assume that the still contains only ethanol and water. Ignoring the azeotrope discussed below, for every mix ratio of ethanol to water there is one and only one new boiling point that lies between the boiling point of either. Conversely, for each boiling point, there is one and only one ratio of ethanol in the kettle, and an enriched ratio in the vapor and the distillate.

Assume a mixt ure of 90% water and 10% ethanol (by volume) is to be separated by distillation. Water has a boiling point of 212° F and ethanol has a boiling point of 173° F, but this 10% ethanol mixture will boil at 197° F; it will not boil at 173° F. The vapor above the liquid will be 61% ethanol, as will the distillate. In a simple kettle, the ethanol percentage will drop during the boil because more ethanol than water is being removed, and neither is being replenished. This alone accounts for the increase in boiling point from start to finish—the ratio changes, so the boiling point changes.

Note that we started with 10% ethanol in the kettle, and now have a distillate at 61% ethanol, a six-fold increase in strength. Referring to the table and graph below, if we now distill this condensate again, the new distillate will be 86%, and if we distill that, we will have a 91%, and again 92%, and again 93% and after six distillations, we may get 94%. As the concentration of the impurity (water) decreases, it becomes more difficult to remove. This notion is very important for other products of fermentation in our wash. No matter what the concentration and boiling point of a given impurity, some of it will escape the kettle and find its way to the distillate throughout the distilling run. This means that heads cuts can never be precise because these lighter impurities do not all vaporize before the hearts begin. Likewise, some tails impurities manage to vaporize well before they are expected to. Compounds with boiling points between water and ethanol, such as diacetyl at 190° F, may be impossible to remove by distillation. Therefore, distilling a bad wash never makes a good whiskey—and a good whiskey always starts with a good wash.

High-separation vodka stills employ a reflux column with many plates where vapors can condense; then, like small kettles, revaporize the new enriched liquid, further enriching the vapor. Multiple cycles of condensation and reboiling, one cycle per plate, occur in a single pass as vapors rise through the column before distillate is drawn from the still at the head. Even these stills can not enrich beyond 96.5% ABV because ethanol and water form an azeotrope where some mix ratios have a boiling point not between the boiling points of the constituents. This prevents complete distillation. Nonetheless, reflux columns attached to a pot still can sharpen separation, making head and tail cuts easier, but most believe that this leads to a lesser whiskey because the cleaner separation strips character. Artisan distillers want to preserve the character of their whiskey, so if a column is employed, the plates are bypassed or removed to reduce reflux and more closely match the results from the neck and arm of a traditional whiskey still.

If your kettle temperature is 198.5° F, then your kettle contains 9% ethanol and the vapor contains 59% ethanol. As the run goes on, ethanol is removed from the kettle, the kettle temperature rises toward 212° F and the vapor concentration decreases.

The Different Types of Stills
There are a number of different designs of stills. The most basic design is a "pot still," with a pipe leading from the lid into a condenser coil. The condenser coil can either be long enough to air-cool the vapors or it can be shorter and immersed in a water jacket. Such a still affords minimum separation, since there is almost no separation of the vapors once they leave the boiler. Although this design of still is not suitable for producing beverage alcohol by modern standards, it will still concentrate an 8 or 10% ABV wash to 60% in a fairly fast run.

The next type of still is the "whiskey still," sometimes called a "gooseneck still." This design is technically a form of pot still, has been in use for centuries for commercial whiskey production and is just as popular in modern whiskey distilleries as it has ever been. A whiskey still has a large boiler with a long, broad neck rising from it. The neck bends at the top and leads to a condenser coil immersed in water. This design is very similar to the crude pot still, except the neck affords enough separation to hold back most of the fusel alcohols from the distillate while retaining the desired flavors in the finished spirit. They are suited to the production of whiskey, brandy, rum, schnapps and other non-neutral spirits, for which they are widely used commercially. However, the whiskey still is not suitable for the production of vodka, gin or other spirits derived from neutral alcohol, which require a high-separation still capable of producing pure ethanol.

This brings us to the high-separation still design called a "column still" or a "fractionating still." A fractionating still is used to produce pure ethanol by fractional distillation for vodka and gin or for pharmaceutical and laboratory use.

In smaller fractionating stills, the vapors emerging from the boiling mixture pass up a column packed with small pieces of glass, ceramic, stainless steel, copper or other material inert to the process. This material is called the "column packing." In larger fractionating stills, the columns have baffle plates with holes or bubble caps instead of packing material. Each piece of packing, or bubble cap, can hold a small amount of liquid, either internally (if they have internal crevices) or in the interstices between adjacent particles. At the top of the column, the emerging vapor is condensed into a liquid by means of a heat exchanger with cold water running through it. The condensed liquid runs back down the column until it reaches the boiler, where it is reheated, converted into vapor once more and once again moves up the column.

At equilibrium, which takes about an hour to achieve in the case of pure-ethanol production, the system consists of vapor rising up the column meeting a flow of liquid running down the column from the heat exchanger. At each vapor–liquid interface on the packing material within the column, a partial separation occurs wherein the more volatile components of the mixture go into the vapor phase and rise while the less volatile components go into the liquid phase and are carried down toward the boiler. At equilibrium, the various components in the mixture become stacked up in the column in the order of their boiling points, the most volatile at the top and the least volatile at the bottom.

There's a variation of fractionating still called the "continuous-run still." With the continuous-run design of fractionating still, the fermented wash is fed into a small boiling chamber from a reservoir and is vaporized immediately upon entry to the chamber. The different components of the mixture are drawn off at various heights along the column, and the spent residue is drained off at the bottom. (Acetone, for example, would be continuously drawn off from the top of the column while ethanol would be continuously drawn off from a point a little farther down.) This process can continue indefinitely as long as fermented wash is fed into the boiling chamber.

The last still design to be discussed in this text is the "reflux still." A reflux still is very similar in design to the fractionating still, except it doesn't have a heat exchanger at the top of the column forcing a complete condensation of all the vapor that reaches the top. It has a packed column like a fractionating still, but the vapor that reaches the top exits to the condenser and is received as output. While a reflux still benefits by the purifying process of the redistilling at the packing surfaces like a fractionating still does, without the forced reflux of a top heat exchanger it doesn't produce as pure a neutral ethanol as a fractionating still. However, reflux stills are very commonly used in the artisan distillation of whiskey and other non-neutral spirits, and it's this type of still that will be discussed in the rest of this text.

Most artisan stills are of the reflux or pot-column design because of the inherent flexibility that they offer. The best-known manufacturers of pot and reflux stills are: Vendome, Holstein, Christian Carl and Forsyth. These brands come with multiple bubble-cap trays, and each tray can be bypassed by operating a lever. These stills can also be purchased with a dephlegmator, which is a chilling apparatus at the top of the column comprising a bank of tubes with cold water running through them to increase the reflux, and therefore the purity of the distillate. The still can be operated with the dephlegmator disabled or with cold water running through it at whatever rate the operator chooses. Between the variability of the dephlegmator and the ability to bypass, or not, the multiple bubble-cap trays, just about any level of separation can be achieved with these artisan stills. That's why they make such excellent whiskey stills.

The Flavor of Shape

The whiskey still has four parts: pot, swan neck, lyne arm and condenser. The shape of each section affects rectification and the taste of the spirits. It can be heated by direct fire, electricity, steam, gas or wood. All systems have advantages and disadvantages. There is no right way to heat wash. Most manufacturers, however, prefer a double-jacketed steam system that provides a gentle heat to the wash. Mainly, you don't want to burn the wash. Most pots have a sight glass so the distiller can check for foaming during the distillation process.

The swan neck sits on top of the pot. It can be tall, short, straight or tapered. Often the swan neck is connected to the pot via an ogee, a bubble-shaped chamber. The ogee allows the distillate to expand, condense and fall back into the pot during distillation. Most pot stills have a tapered swan neck, allowing for better separation and better enriching of the spirits during distilling.

The lyne arm sits on top of the swan neck. It can be tilted up or down, and it can be tapered or straight. Most arms are tapered down. Often pot stills are fitted with a dephlegmator, or what the Scots call a "purifier." The dephlegmator is fitted with baffles that use water plates or tubes to cool the distillate, sending 90% of it back to the pot. Its main purpose is the enrichment of the spirit before it's sent on to the condenser.

The condenser, or worm, is used for cooling and condensing the spirit vapor and providing a small stream to a collection tank or pail.

Distillation Process
In distilling parlance, the compounds in the wash that are not ethanol or water are called congeners. Some congeners such as acetaldehyde, methanol and certain esters and aldehydes, have boiling points lower than ethanol, while certain other esters, the higher alcohols (fusel alcohols) and water have higher boiling points than ethanol. This means the lower-boiling-point congeners come out in high concentration at the beginning of the distillation run, and the higher-boiling-point ones come out in high concentration toward the end of the run, leaving the ethanol as the most abundant compound during the middle of the run.

So, when distillation takes place in an artisan still, such as the reflux stills discussed above, the distillate that comes out is divided into three phases called heads, hearts and tails. The heads contain the unwanted lower-boiling-point congeners that come out at the beginning of the run, and the tails contain the unwanted higher-boiling-point congeners that come out at the end of the run. The hearts are the desired spirit.

Since whiskey is not distilled at a high-separation level, each phase bleeds into the adjacent phase. That is to say, there's a considerable amount of ethanol in the heads phase, and there are late-heads congeners at the beginning of the hearts phase. Similarly, there's a significant amount of early-tails congeners at the end of the hearts, and there's a considerable amount of ethanol in the tails phase. The hearts are the whiskey, and while they are composed mostly of ethanol and water, they have a delicate balance of late-heads and early-tails congeners that make up the flavor profile of the whiskey.

Since both the heads and the tails contain a lot of ethanol and residual desirable flavor, they are mixed together and saved for future recovery. The heads and tails when mixed together are called feints. They can be distilled separately to produce another whiskey run or they can be mixed in with a future spirit run, where their ethanol and flavors are recovered as a part of that run. However, each subsequent distillation produces its own set of heads, hearts and tails, and the feints from those runs are also saved for future recovery.

When whiskey is made, it's usually done in two distillation runs: a beer-stripping run and a spirit run. The beer-stripping run is generally done in a larger, high-volume pot still called a beer stripper. The beer stripper is used to distill the fermented mash and concentrate the ethanol and all the impurities into a distillate of about 35% ethanol, called "low wines." The spirit run is done in a smaller whiskey still, either a gooseneck or an artisan reflux still, called a "spirit still." The spirit still is used to distill the low wines and refine them into the finished spirit. There are two outputs retained from the spirit run: the finished spirit and the feints.

For a beer-stripping run, the fermented mash, which is typically about 8% ABV, is loaded into the beer-stripper and the contents are brought to boil. Since this run is just a primary distillation, the heads, hearts and tails are not separated out. The entire output from this run is collected in a single lot, and the run is continued until the aggregate percent alcohol is down to 35% ABV. This distillate is the low wines, which is the input to the spirit run.

To produce the finished whiskey, the spirit still is filled with the low wines from the beer-stripping run and often a measure of feints from previous spirit runs. The spirit still is then brought to a boil. It is with the spirit run that the distiller adjusts the boil-up rate to achieve a gentle, slow flow of distillate and carefully separates out the heads, hearts and tails.

Some whiskey distilleries produce their whiskey in one single distillation. In effect, they do a spirit run directly from the wash. The artisan reflux stills discussed above are excellently suited to this type of whiskey distillation, but operationally it's very labor-intensive and a lot of attention must be paid by the distiller to numerous smaller runs rather than one larger run.

Some people find the whiskey from a single distillation run to be richer and to have a more natural flavor, while others find it to be harsh and unrefined. In this text, the more common double-distillation method is used.

Making the Cuts

Probably the most elusive part of the distilling process for making whiskey is making the cuts from heads to hearts and then to tails. Making a cut from one phase to the next is the point where the distiller switches the output so that it is collected in a different receiver than the previous phase. At the end of the spirit run, the heads will be in one container, the hearts in another and the tails in a third one. The question is: When to switch from one phase to the next?

Experienced distillers do this by taste. Even though there are measurable parameters, like still-head temperature and percent alcohol of the evolving spirit, that can be used to judge when to make the cuts, taste and smell remain the most reliable factors in determining them.

The empirical parameters for judging the cuts are: the percent alcohol of the spirit that's flowing out of the still (i.e., the evolving spirit) and the still-head temperature. However, these vary from one still to the next and vary based on the properties of the low wines (e.g., percent alcohol and quantity). It is possible to develop a consistent process using the same still and the same quantity and a formulation of low wines, such that the parameters remain the same for each run. For example, if a spirit run is being done in an artisan reflux still with low wines of 35% ABV, the begin-cut (i.e., the cut from heads to hearts) is usually done when the evolving distillate is at about 80% and when the still-head temperature is about 180° F. The end-cut (i.e., the cut from hearts to tails) is often done at about 65% and when the still-head temperature is about 200° F. However, a spirit distilled from a straight malt wash can often be end-cut as low as 60%. It's because of these nuances that smell and taste become the only truly reliable indicators of when to make the cuts.

When making the begin-cut, the taste characteristics that the distiller is looking for are as follows. When a spirit run comes to boil and the first distillate starts flowing from the still, this is the beginning of the heads phase. The distiller can collect a small sample of the distillate on a spoon or in a wine glass and smell it. At this stage, the distillate will have the sickening smell of solvents like nail polish remover or turpentine. However, before long this solvent smell will diminish, and even when a sample is tasted these compounds will be very faint. As the solvent character disappears completely, the distillate will start to take on a hint of whiskey flavor. This flavor will increase until it becomes very pronounced and highly concentrated. It's when this flavor is clearly evident (i.e., more than just a hint) but is still increasing in intensity that the distiller cuts to the hearts phase.

To make the end-cut, the distiller needs to monitor the flavor of the hearts through the following changes in taste. At the beginning of the hearts phase, the intensity of the whiskey flavor will still be increasing and will continue to do so until it becomes very strong. However, as the hearts continue, the intense whiskey flavor will fade into a smooth, sweet, pleasant flavor that will persist for most of the hearts. The flavor will change slightly as the hearts progress but it will remain sweet and pleasant. Toward the end of the hearts, the flavor will start losing its sweetness and a trace of harsh bitterness will begin to appear in the flavor. This harsh, bitter flavor is the onset of the tails. While a small amount of this bitterness is considered to contribute to the "bite" character of the whiskey, the distiller should cut to the tails receiver before much of it is allowed to enter the hearts.

The tails can be collected until the evolving distillate is down to about 10% and the still-head temperature is about 210° F. The reason for doing this is to render all the residual alcohol that's left in the still at the end of the hearts phase. This alcohol can then be recovered in a future spirit run.

The tails phase starts out bitter and the bitterness becomes more intense as the tails continue. But as the tails progress, the bitterness subsides and gives way to a sweet-tasting water. This sweet water is called "backins."

Background

Whiskey in North America is distilled in two different ways. One is by continuous distillation in a column still, and the other is by an intermittent process in batch stills. Batch stills are stills that have a kettle that is filled with a fixed quantity of the substrate to be distilled (i.e., a batch). There are basically two methods of pot distillation.

Method One

Two distillation runs are done using the same still for both runs. The still is run with the plates open, and a primary distillation is done on all the wash. This run produces low wines of 25 to 55% ABV, depending on the alcohol of the wash and speed of the run.

Then a spirit run is done on the low wines produced by the primary distillation, using the same still with one plate down to produce a yield at 70 to 75% ABV. This is watered back to 60% ABV and barreled.

Method Two

The two distillations are done in separate special-purpose stills, namely a "wash still" and a "spirit still." The wash is distilled in the wash still to produce low wines of 25 to 55% ABV. The low wine is then distilled in the spirit still to 70 or 75% ABV. This is watered back to 60% ABV for barreling.

Beer Stripping

The first step in distilling whiskey is to do a crude primary distillation of the wash called a beer-stripping run. The output of a beer-stripping run is called low wines, which are then input to the final distillation (i.e., the spirit run), which produces the finished whiskey. The purpose of beer stripping is to concentrate the alcohol and the congeners in the wash into a substrate of about 35% ABV.

To do a beer-stripping run, the still is loaded and the heat is applied to the boiler. When the wash comes to boil, the heat should be adjusted to deliver a fast flow rate into the receiver. For a stripping run, there's no need to separate out heads, hearts and tails. The idea is to simply do a fast, crude primary distillation on the wash.

Initially, the percent alcohol of the aggregate distillate in the receiver will be well over 80% ABV, but as the run progresses, the alcohol percentage will drop. The beer-stripping run is to be continued until the aggregate distillate drops down to 25% ABV. At this point, the still-head temperature will be close to 212° F.

> Note: The percent alcohol to be monitored here is the entire aggregate of distillate in the receiver—not the percent alcohol of the evolving spirit as measured at the parrot.

When the distillate is down to 25% ABV, the still can be shut down and the residue drained. Repeat this process on the remaining wash.

When the entire batch of wash has been stripped, you will be ready to proceed to the spirit-run step.

Spirit Run

The spirit run is the final distillation that produces the finished whiskey. It's done in a spirit still and must be performed carefully at the proper heat level and flow rate, with the correct bubble-cap trays selected and with special attention being paid to the begin- and end-cuts to ensure a proper separation of heads, hearts and tails.

To do a spirit run, the spirit still is loaded with low wines, the required bubble-cap trays are enabled, steam heat is applied to the boiler and the flow should be set to the heads receiver. When the wash comes to a boil, the steam pressure should be adjusted to the correct level for running whiskey.

Initially, the percent alcohol of the distillate at the parrot will be close to 90% ABV and the spirit run will be in its heads phase. The distillate will be set to flow into the heads receiver at this point. As the run progresses, the percent alcohol at the parrot will decrease. It's important that the distiller takes a small sample of the distillate every few minutes and smells and tastes it. At first, the distillate will smell of acetaldehyde and other pungent chemical-like smells. When such smells are evident, it's not necessary to taste the spirit. As the distillation continues, this chemical-like smell will diminish and the percent alcohol at the parrot will decrease.

After a short while, the chemical-like smell will no longer be evident, and there will be only a faint taste of it. A little while later, the distillate will smell and taste almost neutral. Shortly after this, the distillate will begin to taste of whiskey, and this flavor will become quite intense. This is the point where the distiller must begin-cut to the hearts phase and set the flow into the hearts receiver. The percent alcohol at the parrot at the begin-cut will be about 80% ABV, and for a distiller not yet familiar with judging the begin-cut by taste, 80% ABV at the parrot is a good empirical measurement with which to judge the begin-cut.

As the distillation progresses, the intense whiskey flavor will subside and the distillate will take on a smooth, pleasant sweetness. This pleasant sweetness will continue but as the percent alcohol decreases, it will become more diluted-tasting. And, as the tails phase approaches, a bitterness will begin to creep into the flavor. Past a certain point, although the distillate will still have a sweetness to it, it will no longer taste pleasant. It's around this point that the distiller should end-cut to the tails phase, and set the flow into the tails receiver. At the end-cut, the percent alcohol at the parrot will be between 60 and 65% ABV. An all-malt whiskey will usually end-cut a little lower than a corn or rye whiskey. It's common for a corn whiskey to end-cut at 64 or 65% ABV, and for an all-malt whiskey to end-cut at 60 or 61% ABV. Again, this empirical measurement is a good indicator by which distillers can judge the end-cut if they are not yet familiar with judging by taste. At the end-cut, the distiller must set the flow into the tails receiver.

The tails phase should be continued until the percent alcohol at the parrot is about 10%. The still-head temperature will be about 212° F, and the still can be shut down and the residue drained. At this point, the heads and the tails can be combined and stored as "feints" for future processing.

Chapter Ten

Seven Steps to Make Award-Winning Whiskey in Your Basement

by Michael Myer, Distillery 291, Colorado Springs, CO

1. The Cook

Creating whiskey is a lot like cooking dinner, with the mash bill being the recipe. Grain types, temperatures and chemistry all affect the outcome. Need: grain, water at a specific temperature and enzymes for starch-to-sugar conversion.

Grain

Decide on the style of whiskey you want to make and source your ingredients.

Your options for sourcing grain as a nano distillery include the local home-brew shop, local brewery and farmers. Often, if you purchase your grain from a homebrew shop, you can mill it at their facility, although most homebrew shops carry only malted grains. If you partner with a brewery, you can order grain through their accounts and potentially mill it on-site with smaller breweries. If you purchase grain from a local farmer, you will need to buy your own drill-driven roller mill.

Examples of grain bills:
Bourbon: 51%+ corn in mash bill
Corn whiskey: 80%+ corn
Rye: 51%+ rye

Water

Water is used to pull the starch out of the grain. Starch extraction occurs differently at different temperatures.

Enzymes

Enzymes that convert starch to sugar occur naturally in malted grains. Malted barley, containing a higher amount of these enzymes, is used regularly as some percent of the mash bill. Starch-converting enzymes can also be bought at your local homebrew shop or online suppliers.

Once you mill your grain into hot water, you'll need to let the mixture rest for around 15–30 minutes. This is when the conversion from starch to sugar happens. There are enzymes to thin the mash, which changes the viscosity of the mash for easier handling.

2. Fermentation temperature, yeast and time

Somewhere around 75–80° F is ideal to pitch yeast in whiskey production. Higher temperatures in beer create off-flavors, but which in whiskey produce depth and character. Too high of a temperature stresses the yeast and causes low ethanol output.

Different strains of yeast create different flavors in your whiskey and different percentages of alcohol by volume.

Your yeast strain and the amount of yeast pitched determine the number of days in your fermentation. Five days is the norm in whiskey production.

3. Stripping run (no cuts)

You are stripping the alcohol and water vapor off the distiller's beer, or wash, reducing the beer wash to a low wine through a stripping still. In the stripping run, you are boiling the beer wash and collecting the alcohol and water vapor. Collect all distillate, no heads or tails cut.

Take an 8–10% ABV beer and reduce the volume to increase the alcohol level to a 35% ABV low wine.

4. Spirits run, heads and tails cuts

Put the 35% ABV low wine in the spirit still and increase the temperature slowly over a long period of time (12 hours) to separate the high alcohol and esters (heads) and the fusel oils and water (tails) from the ethanol (hearts).

5. Barrel-aging

Dilute your hearts distillate to 60% ABV for aging in charred American white oak barrels. Depending on the size of your still, you will have to save the hearts from several runs to collect enough to fill a barrel (e.g., filling a 55-gallon barrel with 60% ABV distillate requires fermenting and distilling about 925 gallons of 8% ABV wash). You can purchase smaller barrels (5, 15 or 30 gallons), although the physics and chemistry of aging in small barrels differs considerably from full-size barrels. Extraction of color and tannins happens much more rapidly (months instead of years) in small barrels, making it easier to get bottles to market quickly. However, because the spirit will have to be removed from a smaller barrel in less time (to avoid over-extraction) and because small barrels have much less surface area than a full-size barrel, little to no mellowing oxidation can occur, resulting in what many consider a more raw or harsh finished spirit.

6. Blending with water to proof
The addition of high-quality water to your finished distillate lowers the ABV to the desired bottling proof.

7. Marketing
Keep it local. With a nano distillery, you can only produce so much whiskey, so you need to focus on the greatest margin of sale. When you get large enough to start distributing, that helps spread awareness of your product and you can make a small profit. Until you reach the growth threshold of distribution, focus on sales of your product direct to consumers through your nano distillery. Focus on social media ad word of mouth to reach the surrounding community. Your brand has to be well-defined, and your marketing disciplined and focused.

The Double-Loop Tote Cooling System

During distillation most craft distillers put the water from the condenser down the drain. To conserve water and save money, you can use a 250-gallon tote as a recirculating cooling system.

Using this basic recirculating system, the water returning from the condenser during distillation will heat the tote water about 30° F. And it will take a day or two for the warm water in the tote to come back down to room temperature (70° F). You have to carefully watch the head temperature of the still because the warming water will affect the distillation process.

To make this system more efficient, you can add a water chiller and recirculate the tote water while the still is running. It will produce enough cold water to keep the tote water at a constant temperature. A water chiller can be purchased from Amazon, eBay or Grainger.com for around $350–$500.

A double-loop water chiller system works like this: The first loop connects the tote water to the condenser and back. The second loop uses a small (½ HP) water pump to run the tote water to the chiller and back. (The photo shows the blue pump that is pumping the chilled water back to the tote.)

With a double-loop tote and condenser-chiller system, you can distill every day because the chiller keeps the cooling water at a constant temperature. Make sure to add a cup of bleach each week to preserve water clarity.

John Reid
Old Flatbed Distillery, Meridian, ID

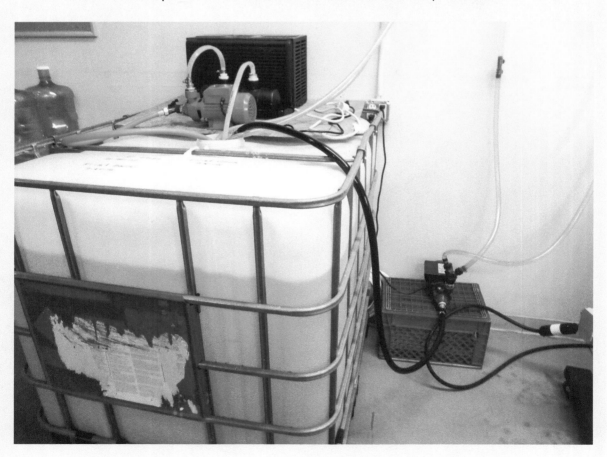

Gin botanicals

Chapter Eleven

Gin Styles and Techniques

Excerpted from *Gin: The StillDragon Way*, available from http://www.stilldragon.com; © Philip Crossley (aka Crozdog), Founder & Distiller at Mobius Distilling Co., Sydney, Australia

History

By the mid-17th century, numerous small Dutch and Flemish distillers (some 400 in Amsterdam alone by 1663) had popularized the re-distillation of malt spirit or wine with juniper, anise, caraway, coriander, etc., which were sold in pharmacies and used to treat such medical problems as kidney ailments, lumbago, stomach ailments, gallstones and gout.

Gin became popular in England after the government allowed unlicensed gin production and at the same time imposed a heavy duty on all imported spirits. This created a market for poor-quality grain that was unfit for brewing beer, and thousands of gin shops sprang up throughout England, a period known as the Gin Craze. Because of the relative price of gin, when compared with other drinks available at the same time and in the same geographic location, gin became popular with the poor. Of the 15,000 drinking establishments in London, not including coffee shops and drinking chocolate shops, over half were gin shops.

In London in the early 18th century, much gin was distilled legally in residential houses (there were estimated to be 1,500 residential stills in 1726) and was often flavored with turpentine to generate resinous woody notes in addition to the juniper. As late as 1913, Webster's Dictionary states without further comment, "'common gin' is usually flavored with turpentine."[1]

Styles/Types

So, what exactly is gin?

In the USA, the TTB Standard of Identity for gin, 27 CFR §5.22(c), reads as follows:

---

1   Source: http://en.wikipedia.org/wiki/gin

Class 3; gin: "Gin" is a product obtained by original distillation from mash, or by redistillation of distilled spirits, or by mixing neutral spirits, with or over juniper berries and other aromatics, or with or over extracts derived from infusions, percolations, or maceration of such materials, and includes mixtures of gin and neutral spirits. It shall derive its main characteristic flavor from juniper berries and be bottled at not less than 80° proof. Gin produced exclusively by original distillation or by redistillation may be further designated as "distilled". "Dry gin" (London dry gin), "Geneva gin" (Hollands gin), and "Old Tom gin" (Tom gin) are types of gin known under such designations.

The European Parliamentary Regulation (EC) No. 110/2008 defines "gin" as follows:

(a) Gin is a juniper-flavoured spirit drink produced by flavouring organoleptically suitable ethyl alcohol of agricultural origin with juniper berries (Juniperus communis L).

(b) The minimum alcoholic strength by volume of gin shall be 37.5 %.

(c) Only natural and/or nature-identical flavouring substances as defined in Article 1(2)(b)(i) and (ii) of Directive 88/388/EEC and/or flavouring preparations as defined in Article 1(2)(c) of that Directive shall be used for the production of gin so that the taste is predominantly that of juniper.[2]

This regulation also defines distilled gin and London Gin.

Distilled Gin
Distilled gin is:
(i) a juniper-flavoured spirit drink produced exclusively by redistilling organoleptically suitable ethyl alcohol of agricultural origin of an appropriate quality with an initial alcoholic strength of at least 96% vol in stills traditionally used for gin, in the presence of juniper berries (Juniperus communis L) and of other natural botanicals provided that the juniper taste is predominant, or

(ii) the mixture of the product of such distillation and ethyl alcohol of agricultural origin with the same composition, purity and alcoholic strength; natural and/or nature-identical flavouring substances and/or flavouring preparations as specified in category 20(c) may also be used to flavour distilled gin.

---

2   Source: http://eurlex.europa.eu/LexUriServ/LexUriServ.do?uri=OJ:L:2008:039:0016:0054:EN:PDF

(b) The minimum alcoholic strength by volume of distilled gin shall be 37.5%.

(c) Gin obtained simply by adding essences or flavourings to ethyl alcohol of agricultural origin is not distilled gin.

London Gin

London Gin is a type of distilled gin:

(i) Obtained exclusively from ethyl alcohol of agricultural origin, with a maximum methanol content of 5 grams per hectolitre of 100% vol. alcohol, whose flavour is introduced exclusively through the redistillation in traditional stills of ethyl alcohol in the presence of all the natural plant materials used,

(ii) the resultant distillate of which contains at least 70% alcohol by vol.,

(iii) where any further ethyl alcohol of agricultural origin is added it must be consistent with the characteristics listed in Annex I(1), but with a maximum methanol content of 5 grams per hectolitre of 100% vol. alcohol,

(iv) which does not contain added sweetening exceeding 0.1 gram of sugars per litre of the final product nor colorants,

(v) which does not contain any other added ingredients other than water,

The minimum alcoholic strength by volume of London gin shall be 37.5%.

The term London gin may be supplemented by the term 'dry.'

Other Styles

Jenever/Genever

Dutch gin is very different from English gin, being made from malted grains, making it somewhat similar to unaged whiskey. They are generally lower proof than other gins, and are often aged for a short time.

Jenever is a juniper-flavored spirit. It is made in a more complicated method that allows for more of the flavors from the original base spirit to come through in the final product. It is less neutral than London Dry Gin and is regularly sold with fruit flavorings—citrus is a popular choice.

It is made by blending two spirits together—1) "moutwijn" (malt wine), which is basically an unaged whiskey made from a mixture of rye, malted barley and wheat that is double- or triple-distilled in a pot still to around 45–50% ABV. It is this malt wine that gives jenever its distinctive flavor; and 2) botanically flavored neutral spirit. The botanically flavored neutral spirit is essentially gin, only using less conventional botanicals such as caraway and aniseed.

The blend of the two spirits is determined by the distillers according to the style they are making—"Jonge," "oude" or "kornwijn."

Jonge Jenever

This lighter style was developed in the 1950s and uses around 5% malt wine with fewer botanicals. It is called "jonge" jenever, as it is a "young" style rather than being lightly aged.

Oude Jenever

Oude jenever contains a minimum of 15% malt wine and will often use more botanicals than the jonge style. More intense botanicals like myrrh and aloe are used to match the heavier malt characteristics from the larger percentage of malt wine used. "Oude" refers to the "old" style of traditional jenever rather than it being an aged spirit.

Kornwijn

The use of a minimum of 51% malt wine makes these jenevers much heavier and richer. They are characterized by complex malt character combined with wood and wine flavors. Korawijn must by law be cask-aged.

Plymouth

Gin produced in Plymouth, England, has its own appellation. It cannot be called Plymouth Gin if it is not made in Plymouth. Plymouth Gin is sweeter than dry gin due to a higher than usual proportion of root ingredients, which bring a more earthy feel to the gin as well as a softened juniper flavor.

Old Tom

Old Tom Gin was very popular during the 18th century and is sweeter than London Dry Gin. At that time, gin production was fairly clandestine and the resulting spirits were often impure, poor quality and harsh. To overcome these problems, gin was sweetened to make it more palatable.

Old Tom is lighter and less intense than jenever, but more viscous and fuller-bodied than dry gin, with a sweetness derived from naturally sweet botanicals, malts or added sugar. It's not as aggressively flavored as dry gin, so some of the more subtle notes don't get overwhelmed by the juniper. The alcohol is also a bit lower.

Old Tom lost its popularity after the column still enabled the production of dry gin. At the time of writing, Hayman's and Ransom are two notable commercial examples of Old Tom Gin available, although the category is making a comeback.

Sloe
Sloe gin is a traditional liqueur made by infusing the fruit of the blackthorn in gin, although modern versions are almost always compounded from neutral spirits and flavorings. Similar infusions are possible with other fruits, such as damsons.

Aged
Aged gin is simply a gin which has been left on oak for a period of time to gain color and develop additional flavor complexities which only oaking can provide. In the USA, aging statements are not allowed on gin labels, and distillers instead use terms like "barrel gin" or "barrel rested," etc.

Contemporary
Opinions vary on what constitutes a "contemporary" gin. Two definitions are:

Gin that has juniper as a main flavor, but with more a pronounced focus on other botanicals, which may include the use of locally sourced or unusual botanicals or a different base spirit which may be made in-house.

Gin whose primary flavor is an emphasis on botanicals other than juniper. While juniper will be present, the gin may be more floral, herbal, spicy or citrus-driven compared to dry gins.

The difference is whether juniper or other botanicals dominate.

Techniques
In very broad terms, there are two ways to make gin: compounding and distilling.

Compounding involves adding essential oils and/or essences to neutral spirit, which is then diluted and bottled. It is regarded as producing lower-quality gin. This technique will not be examined further here.

There are two methods for distilling gin: macerating and vapor infusion.

Maceration involves soaking botanicals in alcohol before the botanicals are strained out and the remaining liquid is redistilled. Some distillers do not strain, but put both the liquid and the botanicals in the still. Many commercial gins are produced by this technique; they are often called "Distilled Gins."

Vapor infusion involves placing botanicals in the path of the vapor coming off the still before the vapor is condensed. The vapor picks up the flavors from the botanicals as it passes by. The resultant product is considered by many to be fresher and more delicate than that produced by maceration. Vapor infusion is also considered to retain higher levels of more volatile aromas than maceration. Bombay Gin is made using vapor infusion on Carter-head stills.

Both maceration and vapor infusion can be used to distill individual botanicals, thereby producing single-ingredient distillates that can be blended to produce gin. Making single-ingredient gins provides the producer with the ultimate control of the quantity of that botanical used.

Making single-ingredient distillates is a good way for novice producers to learn about the flavors and aromas of each botanical, and allows experimentation with blending different botanical ratios to be performed.

Ingredients
Spirit
A clean ethanol base is required to make gin. Many commercial operations purchase neutral grain spirit (NGS). Licenses are required to purchase GNS in most countries.

Most gins, apart from jenever, will use the hearts cut of a neutral spirit run as their base.

This hearts cut may be carbon-filtered to provide a very clean and neutral base. Various producers are using spirit which still has the base ingredient character (e.g., grain or grape) present to provide another layer of complexity.

An all-grain barley mash and subsequent distillation(s) will be needed to create the "malt wine" which provides jenever its characteristic flavor. Detailed instructions on all-grain brewing are beyond the scope of this chapter; however, please refer to the Recipe Suggestions section for a basic process.

Botanicals

The three main botanicals used to produce gin are juniper berries, coriander seed and angelica. However, there are hundreds of different botanicals that can be used. The producers are limited only by their imaginations—and what they can source.

As per the definition above, juniper is the only botanical ingredient necessary for the product to be called gin. Yet coriander seed also plays a large role by providing most of the citrus flavors and balancing the juniper.

Typically, between 6 and 12 different botanicals are used. As gin is typically mixed for consumption, flavors will tend to be lost if more than 10 botanicals are used, proving that sometimes "less is more." Gins with large botanical bills employ a "lots of more" approach, that is, they use small amounts of a large number of botanicals to provide layers of complexity.

The following describes characteristics that several of the common botanicals provide.

Almond

Almond provides a marzipan, nutty, spicy flavor. It provides a balancing smoothness that binds all the other ingredients together. Both the bitter and sweet almond can be used. If nuts are used, they have to be ground into a powder before distillation.

Bitter almonds may be hard to locate due to their cyanide content. For the sake of safety, it is recommended that they are avoided where possible. Bitter almond essence can be substituted—it can be found at gourmet food suppliers or occasionally in the cake supplies section of the supermarket—but make sure you don't buy an artificial essence.

While some have reportedly used apricot or peach kernels as a bitter almond substitute, the author cannot comment on or recommend this practice.

Angelica root

An aromatic root with musky, nutty, woody, sweet flavor and a piney, dry sharpness. It provides an earthy backbone, balancing the freshness of juniper, lemon peel and coriander seeds while also fixing and marrying the volatile flavors of other botanicals, giving length and substance by fleshing out the mid-palate.

Aniseed
Aniseed has a fragrant, licorice taste.

Cassia
It gives a warm, delicate, spicy cinnamon note due to a higher coumarin content than normal cinnamon (they are related plants, but not the same). Used to help balance the overall flavor and aroma rather than as a primary flavor.

Cinnamon
Used sparingly to provide background heat.

Coriander seed
Provides the up-front lemon/citrus fresh aroma as well as providing mellow spicy, ginger and sage notes.

Cubeb
Provides a spicy lemon-pine flavor similar to black pepper but with a more floral (lavender, geranium and rose) aroma. It also provides a dry, slightly hot flavor which results in the lively peppery characteristics.

Grains of paradise
Provide a hot, spicy, peppery flavor with hints of lavender, elderflower, chocolate, citrus and mint. Its use intensifies the flavoring effects of all the other botanicals and lasts into the finish.

Juniper
By law this is the main flavor element in gin. The use of juniper delivers a fragrant, piney, evergreen odor and taste. It has a fragrant, spicy, bittersweet taste with overtones of lavender and camphor with a peppery finish. Can sometimes smell slightly of turpentine.

Lemon peel
Only the zest or colored portion of the peel is used to impart the strong citrus astringency that gives gin its fresh, light, clean aroma and taste. Use sparingly and try to use dried versions. The oils from fresh peel have really great variability, meaning it can be hard to get a consistent product.

Licorice
This dried root is used for its well-known flavor, very similar to aniseed. Its use adds a warm sweetness and a faint anise aroma while balancing other botanicals and fixing some volatiles.

Nutmeg
Used sparingly to provide a musky flavor and aroma.

Orange peel
The peel of both bitter and sweet oranges is used; bitter to lend astringency similar to lemons, while sweet gives an impression of sweetness. As with lemon peel, use sparingly and try to use dried versions.

Orris root
Orris is the root of the Florentine iris. It has a very floral, perfumed flavor and has an aroma of violets, earth and cold tea. It is very hard and requires heavy grinding into a powder before use. It is traditionally considered as a fixative for the flavors and aromas of the other botanicals.

Rosemary
Leaves are used for their stimulating and refreshing savory aromas. Typically found in Mediterranean styles.

In addition to these commonly used botanicals, the following are also commonly used. Please note that this list is not exhaustive.

Botanical, Influence
Rose, floral
Hibiscus, floral
Basil, floral, spice
Lemongrass, floral, spice
Ginger, spice, heat
Cardamom, spice
Cumin, spice, heat
Fennel seed, spice
Caraway, spice
Anise, spice
Star anise, spice
Clove, spice
Savory, spice
Chamomile, floral, spice
Pepper (cracked), spice
Lavender, floral
Violet root, floral
Grapefruit peel, citrus
Vanilla, floral, spice

Honeysuckle, floral, spice
Pomelo (Chinese grapefruit), citrus

Individual Maceration[3]

Before attempting to formulate your own recipe, it is beneficial (but not essential) to take some time to research the different botanicals to understand what they contribute to the finished product.

You might like to do small macerations of each individual botanical to gain first-hand knowledge of each botanical. This is simple to do and will assist in developing your palate.

You will need the following:

Small sealable jars—1 per botanical
Botanicals
Mortar & pestle
Vodka (40% ABV)
Measuring cup
Measuring spoons
Labels
Pen
Cupboard space
Notebook for keeping records
Teaspoon
Water

1. Clean and dry all jars (ensure they do not smell of the previous contents if reusing).

2. Measure 50 ml vodka into each jar

3. One by one, measure out 0.5 to 1 teaspoon of each botanical. Crush each botanical in mortar and pestle, then add to one of the jars. Screw lid on firmly. Label jar with the name of the botanical and make an entry in your notebook. Repeat for other botanicals. For the citrus fruits, simply peel off some and put in a jar with vodka. There is no need to crush powdered ingredients like orris root.

4. Shake each jar well.

5. Place in a cupboard & shake each day for 2–10 days.

---

3   Based on the gin-tasting technique of Aaron Knoll at the *Gin is In*, http://theginisin.com/our-philosophy/a-new-way-to-review-gin/]

6. Once you can't wait any longer, remove the jars from the cupboard and line them up on a bench or table.

7. Find the record sheet with the names of each botanical.

8. Take the first jar give it a shake before opening.

9. When you open it, smell the contents—don't poke your nose right in the jar, but hold the jar under your nose and a little in front. Use your hand to waft the aroma from the jar to your nose.

10. Record your aroma impressions in your notebook.

11. Take a teaspoon and fill it half-full from the jar. Add some water to the teaspoon before tasting.

12. Record your taste impressions. What do you taste? Where do you taste it? Is there any aftertaste? What if you water it down some more?

13. Cleanse your palate with fresh water and plain crackers before evaluating the next sample.

The following chart describing flavors found in gin will assist your evaluation (The information is categorized by the Scotch Whiskey Research Institute).

Nasal Effects	Pungent
	Alcohol Burn
Juniper	Pine
	Grass
	Herbaceoous/Waxy
	Woody/Resinous
Citrus	Lemon Peel
	Orange Peel
	Zesty
Green	Herbal
	Grassy
	Leafy
	Pine
Spicy	Dried Spice
	Cinnamon
	Coriander Seed
	Peppery

Table continues on next page

Aniseed	Licorice
	Aniseed
Sweet	Vanilla
	Honey
Floral	Fragrant
	Perfumed
	Fresh Flowers
Fruit	Artificial Fruit Flavorings
	Fresh Fruit
Nutty	Marzipan
	Almond
Off-Notes	Solvent
	Oily
	Sulphury
	Sour
	Musty/Earthy

When tasting, be aware how your sense of taste works:

Firstly, a large part of taste comes from the aromas detected by your nose; your tongue provides direct taste (1), while trigeminal effects (2), retronasal (3) and aftertaste (4) all play their own parts.

A list of botanical suppliers can be found in the American Distilling Institute Directory.

Recipe Formulation[4]
Radar Charts*
One technique to consider when developing a recipe is to think about what you want the resultant product to be in terms of its intensity of five flavor/aroma elements:

Juniper—The base note intensity. Don't forget that pine/camphor/lav-

---

4   Based on the gin tasting technique of Aaron Knoll at the Gin is In, http://theginisin.com/our-philosophy/a-new-way-to-review-gin/]

ender notes derive from juniper.
Citrus—Lemon, lime, grapefruit, etc.
Spice—The warm mouthfeel and depth of earthy elements.
Heat—Alcohol "burn" combined with the ingredient mouthfeel.
Floral—Self-explanatory.

You can photocopy this chart to plot out how you want the end product to be. Once your plot is complete, consider which ingredients will provide you with what you envisage.

You can also use this technique when evaluating your final product. The use of this technique over time will build up your personal library of reference data that will allow you to not only see how the botanicals contribute to the end result, but enable you to make informed decisions.

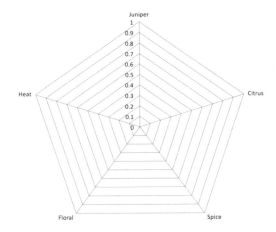

Fixatives

Do not forget the important role that "fixatives" perform in gin. Apart from the flavor and aroma contribution they provide, orris root and angelica root are used as fixatives for preserving the flavors and aromas of the other chosen botanicals. They act much like Velcro and hold everything together. Without the use of fixatives, over time the floral notes will dominate as the juniper and citrus character will disappear.

Ingredient Proportions

Whereas gin must be a juniper-based spirit, coriander seed is the second most important botanical. These two botanicals typically constitute up to 90% of the botanicals used. The ratio of juniper to coriander will depend on the style that you are trying to produce. An "assertive" gin will have a higher proportion of juniper to coriander seed (e.g. ,10:1), while softer more "delicate" gins will use less juniper—sometimes much less (even down to 1:1). You would use a lower ratio if you wanted your product to highlight the notes of other subtler botanicals.

Once you have determined the juniper-to-coriander ratio, you can then focus on determining what other ingredients to use and their quantity based on what flavors or characteristics you would like to appear.

A Rough Rule of Thumb

If you spend any time researching gin recipes, you will quickly discover that everyone has their own idea on how much of each botanical to use and the ratio(s) between them. That, combined with the fact that most of the recipes available are for the maceration technique, makes the process of determining botanical quantities (or ratios) for vapor-infused gin quite challenging.

To overcome that hurdle, we've developed the following table as a guide to provide you with indicative proportions to start your journey of developing your own gin flavors.

Be aware that what follows is a theoretical guide, as the freshness and quality of botanicals able to be sourced will differ. Oil content is incredibly variable. Large gin distilleries have departments dedicated to analyzing botanical oil content to ensure product consistency. One person may be able to source fresh, pungent Albanian juniper berries, while someone else has to make do with whatever is on the local spice-shop shelf. You will therefore need to work out what works best for you based on what you can source. Changing the source of your botanicals will impact your finished product.

Flavoring Level	Botanical	Juniper Flavoring Ratio	Example
Primary	Juniper	1	100 g
Secondary	Coriander seed	10:1 to 1:1[*]	From 10-100 g
Tertiary	Angelica root, cassia, cinnamon, licorice, bitter almond, grains of paradise, cubeb berries	Up to 8:1	Up to 12.5 g of each botanical

Quaternary	Bitter orange peel, sweet orange peel, ginger, orris root, cardamom, nutmeg, savory, chamomile, lemon peel, cracked pepper, lavender, etc.	Up to 80:1	Up to 1.25 g of each botanical

*Note: Botanicals used from the same flavoring level do not need to be added at the same rate (e.g., you may use 5 g licorice but only 2 g angelica).

The use of ratios allows you to easily scale your recipes to match the quantity of spirit you want to produce. As a guide, use between 25 and 40 g of botanicals per liter of spirit, (e.g., use between 150 and 240 g total botanicals in a 6-L "all-in-one" batch). The use of fewer botanicals and more spirit will result in a "lighter" end product.

[Editor's Note: Scaling of botanical quantities and ratios with batch size is a highly subjective undertaking once the amount of spirit involved exceeds more than 10 liters or so. As batch size increases, the required amount of each botanical does not necessarily scale linearly, and the respective ratios can change. Careful, incremental experimentation is required to achieve the desired flavor profile.]

Distillation
A Carter head is an add-on to a column or pot still that is designed in such a way that the alcohol-laden vapor is forced through a basket (or baskets) loaded with botanicals. As the vapor passes the botanicals, numerous flavor and aroma compounds are extracted. The enriched vapor is then directed to the condenser where it is cooled, converting it back into a liquid.

StillDragon[5] produced one of the first off-the-shelf Carter-head units for use by both distillers of all sizes.

While it is possible to produce gin directly from a wash by inserting the botanicals into the vapor path after the heads cuts, this is not recommended. You will get a higher-quality product more consistently by using diluted high-quality

5   StillDragon sells modular distillation equipment globally: In the USA, Canada and South America, visit http://stilldragon.com/. In Asia, Australia, New Zealand and the Pacific, visit http://www.stilldragon.com.au/. In Europe and Africa, visit https://www.stilldragon.eu/en/.]

neutral spirit in the boiler. Doing a direct wash-to-product run or a low wines-to-product run would require making cuts on the fly, which as we know is difficult, and may not extract all of the character from the botanicals.

Different flavors will emerge at different stages of the run. Think of the run and flavors as being treelike. The fruitier floral notes found higher in a tree will come out first while the lower, earthier root-like flavors will appear later in a run. However, some ingredients are "ghosts"—they have early extraction, then late extraction.

Method 1: Blending Single-Ingredient Distillations

This method produces a distillate of each individual botanical, which you then blend together using your chosen ratio to obtain a finished product.

You will need to perform a full run per ingredient so you capture every aspect of the botanical in the resulting distillate.

Although it is time-consuming and requires some preparation, individual ingredient runs provide the base distillates that will allow you to experiment with many different blend permutations prior to committing to an all-in-one run.

Product consistency is a key feature of most commercial products. Large commercial operators adjust their ingredient proportions based on chemical analysis of their supplies. That is not feasible for the small operator. Single-ingredient runs provide a mechanism for smaller distillers to adjust the ingredient ratios of their all-in-one runs when new batches of ingredients arrive or a new supplier is used.

You may be tempted to charge the boiler with a large volume of NGS, then periodically put the still into full reflux and change the basket with a different botanical. That is possible, however, it is not recommended, as a full run of each botanical is required to obtain the full flavor. This is because the flavor profile of each botanical changes over the course of a run as temperatures rise and the concentration of alcohol changes. Each botanical's flavor extraction profile differs; some are dominant at the start, with nothing in the middle of the run and more coming out at the end.

Once you have collected jars of each botanical distillate, and prior to blending different distillates together, use radar charts and the rough rule of thumb (above) to determine how much of each of the collected botanical extracts to mix together to produce your final gin.

This technique allows you to quickly experiment with creating product using different ratios of the individual botanical distillations.

Consider making 30-ml blends. Why?

> 1. 30 ml is the size of a standard nip, and if you don't like it, you haven't wasted a lot of extract.

> 2. Errors can be fixed by adding more of other botanical extracts to restore balance.

> 3. Many variations and permutations can be quickly developed without wasting a lot of time or materials such as would occur if the operator mixed a large quantity of various extracts or put a lot of botanicals in the basket and did a full run.

Copy the "Individual Maceration Record Sheet" located in the Appendix. Determine the ratio, then calculate the volume of each extract required in a 30-ml blend. Record details on the record sheet.

After you have allowed the individual distillates to sit overnight, use a pipette to carefully measure the required volume of each extract into a sampling glass and stir well.

Critically evaluate your creation. Swirl and smell. Sip then slowly breathe in through your mouth over the spirit. Swirl the spirit around your mouth, then breathe out of your nose for retronasal evaluation.

How does it compare to how you visualized it tasting? Is it like the radar plot? Does anything dominate? What is lacking? Is it what you anticipated? What else could it use (spice/heat/floral/citrus)?

Take copious tasting notes of the ratios used as well as the aroma and flavor profiles. Mid-palate weight is a key aspect to look for.

If you used radar plots as part of the recipe/ratio formulation, how does the finished blend match the original radar plot? What needs tweaking? Is one aspect dominant or subdued?

If you didn't initially use a radar plot, why not use one as part of your product evaluation?

Adjust the proportions and repeat the process until you have found your perfect ratio.

Now you have the ratio, it is just a simple matter of blending the botanical extracts together in a larger quantity using your perfect ratio to produce the desired volume.

Method 2: All in One

All-in-one runs differ because flavor molecules can bond and form new, complex compounds that individual macerations or single-ingredient runs cannot replicate. This approach builds upon the knowledge gained from blending individual-ingredient distillates without having to make and blend individual extracts. It simply involves loading all of the botanicals into the basket and performing the run.

Once you decide on a ratio, calculate the required weight of each botanical required based on the volume of spirit.

1. Determine the ratio and quantity of each botanical required.

2. Weigh out each botanical and place in a mixing bowl.

3. Mix the botanicals together, then add them to the basket. Hold the basket over the mixing bowl so you don't get powdered ingredients everywhere.

4. Insert the basket in the head and clamp it up.

5. If you run an electric boiler, fill the boiler with water to more than cover the element.

6. Charge the boiler with NGS (amount is dependent on batch size).

7. Top up the boiler with water to reduce the percent ABV to below 40%.

8. Run the still with no reflux.

9. Collect the first 10–20 ml (more in a larger run) in a jar and set aside.

10. Collect all other product down to 10–20%. It is up to you whether you collect in one large jar or many smaller ones and blend later.

11. Shut down the still.

12. Drain the liquid from the Carter head into a waste jar using the drain valve on the bottom of the head.

13. Clean up.

Cuts: Are They Required?

You will note that step 9 above is the collection of a small portion at the start of the run. This isn't a fores or heads cut, rather it will contain an extremely high concentration of botanical extracts—particularly juniper. Some distillers find this to be overpowering and that it can cause louching. It is up to the individual distiller if to decide if this portion is discarded or retained and blended into the rest of the run output.

The process described above is written from the perspective of charging the boiler with the highest-quality neutral spirit possible (e.g., the hearts cut of a neutral run which may have been carbon filtered). As the input spirit quality used in this scenario is so high, a tails cut is not required.

Depending on whether you are macerating directly in the boiler or using a botanical basket for vapor extraction, a tails cut may be necessary to maintain a high-quality spirit. As the run progresses and the temperature of the still rises, some botanicals can begin to produce undesirable flavors. Many commercial distillers will stop gin collection when the still output falls below a certain threshold, from as high as 60% ABV for some, down to 30% ABV for others. Experimentation is required here to determine the appropriate cutoff for your product.

Dilution

Gin is typically diluted to 40–45% ABV, with 42% commonly used. Use quality, filtered spring or distilled water to dilute your spirit to your desired drinking strength. By ensuring the boiler charge is around 18–20%, the combined output will be close to bottling strength. Experimentation is needed to determine the exact charge required to meet individual requirements.

Resting

All newly made gin will benefit from a period of resting before consumption. Resting is simply the process of leaving the diluted/mixed gin for a period of time to allow the flavors to blend together. Resting for 7–21 days before consumption is common.

Evaluation

If you used radar plots as part of the recipe/ratio formulation, how does the finished product match the original radar plot? Does anything need tweaking in the next run? Is one aspect dominant or subdued?

If you didn't initially use a radar plot, why not use one as part of your product evaluation?

Recipe Suggestions

The suggestions below will provide you with a good starting point on your gin journey. You will note that they are all based on ratios that total 100%, which makes the math easier.

The tables also provide minimum and maximum quantities based on a suggested botanical usage rate of between 25 and 40 grams per liter of spirit. Decide on the usage rate you want, multiply that by the batch size and that is how much of each botanical you need to weigh out.

Remember: These quantities are only a guide. It is often more convenient to round the value up to the nearest whole number—for example, you may calculate that you need 9.5 g of grains of paradise, but for convenience it may be easier to measure out 10 g.

London Dry Gin

#1

Botanical	Ratio (%)	Min/Liter (g)	Max/Liter (g)
Juniper	60%	15	24
Coriander	30%	7.5	12
Cassia	5%	1.25	2
Angelica root	5%	1.25	2

#2

Juniper	55%	13.81	22.1
Coriander	28%	6.91	11.05
Cassia	6%	1.38	2.21
Angelica root	6%	1.38	2.21
Licorice	6%	1.38	2.21
Bitter orange peel	1%	0.14	0.22

#3

Juniper	62%	15.43	24.69
Coriander	31%	7.72	12.35

Angelica root	6%	1.54	2.47
Bitter orange peel	1%	0.15	0.25
Orris root	1%	0.15	0.25

#4			
Juniper	47%	11.85	18.96
Coriander	24%	5.92	9.48
Angelica root	5%	1.18	1.9
Cassia	5%	1.18	2.21
Licorice	5%	1.18	2.21
Bitter almonds	5%	1.18	2.21
Grains of paradise	5%	1.18	2.21
Cubeb berries	5%	1.18	2.21
Bitter orange peel	1%	0.12	0.19
Orris root	1%	0.12	0.19

Jenever

To make jenever, you first need to make malt wine (moutwijn). This is achieved by mashing equal amounts of rye, corn and malted barley. For an excellent introduction to all-grain brewing, go to John Palmer's excellent site, www.how-tobrew.com. If you are new to all-grain brewing, also research "brew in a bag," also known as BIAB.

The basic process outlined below is a summary of information sourced from http://www.stillcooker.com.

Equal amounts of rye, corn and malted barley are ground into a coarse grist, then a step-mash is performed with an initial liquid-to-grain ratio of 2:1 as follows:

55° C for 30 minutes
65° C for 60 minutes (the temperature is raised by adding more hot water)
72° C for 30 minutes

At the end of the mash, your drained wort will have a starting gravity (SG) of 1050–1060. Cool the wort to around 25° C and pitch the yeast. The resulting wash will be about 5–7% ABV. Typically, three pot-still distillation runs were used to produce malt wine at about 46–48% ABV. However, that can be cut back to one run using a fractionating still with plates.

To convert malt wine to jenever, malt wine is traditionally divided into four different volumes: One volume remains pure malt wine; the second volume is redistilled in a small pot still loaded with juniper berries; the third part is redistilled to 75% ABV and the fourth part is redistilled with the remaining botanicals. The amounts of each of these four parts is what differentiates each jenever brand.

To replicate this traditional process using a column still with a Carter head, use the following process:

1. Mash and ferment the grains as described above.

2. Configure the still with three or four plates.

3. Charge the boiler with wort, and run.

4. Make cuts as usual,

5. Divide the resulting distillate into two parts:

a. The first part = 1/4 of the total volume at 75% ABV.

b. The second part = 3/4 of the volume at around 47% ABV. You may need to dilute to achieve this.

6. Retain 1/3 of volume of the 47% malt wine and set aside.

7. Charge the boiler with the remaining 2/3 of 47% ABV malt wine.

8. Top up the boiler with water to reduce the % ABV to below 40% and ensure the element does not run dry.

9. Load desired quantity of juniper into one basket and the remaining botanicals in the second basket.

10. Put the basket of juniper in the Carter head and seal it.

11. Collect one volume of juniper-infused malt wine and set aside.

12. Put still into full reflux.

13. Drain the liquid from the Carter head into a waste jar using the drain valve on the bottom of the head.

14. Load the second basket of botanicals into the head and clamp it up.

15. Flush the output path with clean, fresh water—drain from the valve on the bottom of the parrot.

16. Adjust the dephlegmator needle valve to stop any reflux.

17. Collect one volume of botanical-infused malt wine.

18. Shut down the still and clean up.

Blending

You will now have four jars of different malt wines:

1. One volume 47% ABV
2. One volume 75% ABV
3. One volume juniper-infused
4. One volume infused with the remaining botanicals

Use the technique in Method 1: Blending Single-Ingredient Distillates to experiment with different blending ratios to create your own signature jenever! Dilute to 38–40% ABV and add 2 g white sugar per liter. Age for several weeks before consumption.

Jenever producers also guard the ratio of botanicals used in their products. According to http://stillcooker.com, the following will provide the distiller with a good starting point for making 5 liters of jenever.

10 g	Juniper berries
5 g	Coriander
2 g	Caraway seed
2 g	Alsem/wormwood (Artemisia absinthium)
2 g	Mugwort/common wormwood (Artemisia vulgaris)
2 g	Blessed thistle
2 g	Angelica root
2 g	Hops
1 g	Cinnamon
1 g	Nutmeg
0.5 g	Allspice
1.5 g	Orange peel
1 g	Orange blossom

Old Tom

You can make an approximation of Old Tom by adding some sugar syrup to a regular dry gin.

Then again, why not experiment with using "sweet" botanicals and creating your very own interpretation?

Sloe Gin

Collect your sloe berries. For every 1 kg berries, you will need 2 L gin and 200–300 g caster sugar (depending on taste). Place berries into container, add sugar and gin. Stir.

Stir once every day until the sugar has all dissolved. After 3–6 months (or more), strain out the sloe berries. These can be used to make a tasty spread that goes well on a cheese board. Filter the liquid before bottling and storage. Ideally age for several months before drinking.

Other fruits such as blackberries can be used.

Chapter Twelve

Cooking Corn Mash at Whiskey Gap

Brandon Egbert

I add water to my Groen pot (kettle) until it is half-full and then turn on the steam. While the water in the kettle is heating, I'm milling the corn. When the water in the kettle reaches 165° F, I turn on the mixer and add 70 lbs. of milled corn, 15 ml of Termamyl SC and 10 ml of Viscoferm enzymes from Novozymes. Within an hour, the corn mash is at a boil, where I hold it for one hour. At the end of the boil, I add cold water to the mash to bring the temperature down to 160° F and then I add 25 ml of SAN Extra L enzyme from Novozymes. In the next couple of hours, the temperature of the mash will continue to cool. At 155° F, I add 10 pounds of milled, two-row malted barley (15% of the grain bill is barley malt). One hour later, I again add cold water to cool it to about 90° F. (Note: During all these stages, the mixer in the pot is running.) At 90° F, I add yeast and transfer the mash to the fermentation barrel. Many recommend fermentation at a lower temperature, but this system works for me. I ferment for 14 days, give or take a few days. Then I transfer the mash to my still and distill it. An excellent book on this subject is *Making Pure Corn Whiskey* by Ian Smiley, and, of course, there are many YouTube videos on making corn whiskey (moonshine).

Making Single Malt Wash Using a Groen Kettle

Add 15 gallons of water to the kettle and heat to 165° F. Add 35 pounds of two-row barley malt to the kettle and turn on the mixer to slow for a few minutes. The mixing of grain with the water will bring the mash temperature down to 150–155° F. (The mash should look like a thin porridge.)

In 30 minutes, the 152° F starch–water mixture will be converted by natural enzymes into a whiskey mash. (It should have an O.G. of 1072.) At this point, start cooling the mash by adding water to fill the 20-gallon kettle. To further cool the mash, let it sit for a few hours or use cold water running through a copper worm. At 70° F, pitch the yeast and ferment for three to four days. The final gravity should be 1010, approximately 8% alcohol. (Again, we advise doing hot fermentations when making malt washes.)

Repeat the above process three times to produce 50–60 gallons of 8% wash. You can now charge the still and do a fast stripping run (no heads or tails are collected). Each run should produce 15 gallons of low wines at 40% ABV. (Stop the stripping run when the head temperature of the still hits 200° F.)

Repeat the above process, doing four more runs to collect 15 gallons at 40 proof, for a total of 60 gallons of low wines.

On the final, slow spirits run, smell and taste the heads as they come off the still. Collect samples and keep notes on the heads. The long hearts run will produce 30+ gallons of 130-proof distillate—enough to fill one barrel.

Mashing and Distilling at Old Flathead

John Reid

My still holds 53 gallons of wash, and a typical run is 40–44 gallons. I found it was easier to cook and ferment in two 20-gallon batches using a Groen kettle rather than one larger batch.

The Process

Add 15 gallons of water to the kettle. The cooking water should be filtered water or well water and free of chlorine. (Yeast doesn't like chlorinated water.) Many distillers soak their corn overnight, making it easier to cook and reach all the starches for converting to fermentable sugars. The water used in the cooking is important, and most cities add at least some chlorine. If you're using city water, let it sit overnight and chlorine will dissipate; or better yet, rent or buy a reverse-osmosis water purification system.

Add 30 pounds of pre-gelatinized corn, which is also sold as flaked, rolled or pressed corn. (At Amazon, you can find a 50-lb bag of rolled corn for $10.99.) Rolled or flaked corn can also be purchased from a homebrew shop in your town. Rolled corn is easy to cook to convert starches into fermentable sugars. I buy pre-ground corn because it eliminates owning a hammer mill and the dust that is created by milling.

Use a cordless drill with a "mixing paddle" for stirring the corn into the water as it heats. (You can get the mixing paddles just about anywhere that sells tools.) Stir every five minutes or so. Use an infrared thermometer ($25) to check the temperature as you dough-in, or mash-in, the corn.

The Groen kettle heats fast, taking about 15 minutes to reach 150° F. At this temperature, add 4 ounces of amylase enzyme to the kettle—otherwise you will make polenta. At 180° F, the amylase will kick in, and you can watch as it breaks down (converts) the corn starches into sugars. Some distillers prefer not to use enzymes, and instead use 10 pounds of malted barley to achieve starch conversion. Many use both. I prefer making a pure corn mash that is not influenced by other grains. The amylase I use is called SEBSTAR HTL and is an awesome, high-temperature product. It costs about $200 for 2½ gallons, but it goes a long way—a 20-lb. cook (mash) takes about 2 ounces of enzyme. Again, there are many videos online and books covering this subject.

Optional—At 190° F, perform an iodine test to verify that the starches have converted.

At 200° F, turn off the kettle. Add 5–7 gallons of water to get your volume up to 22+ gallons. Allow the mash to cool and settle.

Tilt the kettle and pour the wash through a 12-inch strainer into a bucket. With a bucket, transfer all the wash to the fermenter. Discard the solids that remain in the bottom of the kettle. The cooked corn can be fed to cattle.

Repeat the process to produce 44 gallons of wash for fermentation.

Allow corn wash, in the fermenter, to cool to 70–80° F before adding yeast. The wash can sit overnight to cool to fermentation temperature. A faster method is to use a copper worm or wort chiller and run cold water through it to cool the wash. (Both ways take hours.) Don't be afraid of the wash going sour. Sour wash makes sweet whiskey.

Fermentation will take two to five days, depending on the temperature of the wash. A wash during fermentation sometimes will heat up as much as 8–10° F. Try to keep it from going over 90° F, as the higher temperatures will produce off-flavors (a 70° F fermentation is best). If fermentation is slow, I suggest on day three pumping the wash back onto itself to aerate the mash and give the yeast a shot of oxygen.

Pump or "charge" the still with 44 gallons of wash and perform two distillations. The first is a stripping run and is done without cutting heads or tails. This will produce what is called the low wines, usually 40% alcohol. The low wines combined with two more runs for the final run is called a "spirits run." Typically, 44 gallons (at 40 proof) should yield about 1 gallon of heads, 7 gallons of hearts and up to 2 gallons of tails. Stop running when the head of the still hits 200° F. You can save the tails and add a small amount to a future run. Collect samples while the still is running. I suggest watching YouTube videos on how to make moonshine. Several demonstrate how to properly collect heads and tails. Use your nose and tongue to learn how to make cuts.

If your still has a column with four or five plates and a dephlegmator, you can do a single pass and produce 80- to 100-proof alcohol, although most distillers believe double-distillation is best for whiskey.

Finally, on my equipment it takes about two hours to cook two batches of corn—enough to fill one 55-gallon fermenter. My electric Groen kettle is single-phase, 240 volts. Most Groen kettles found on eBay are 3-phase, but you can buy a phase converter for about $100 and convert if a 3-phase kettle is not available. (Hire an electrician.)

Making "Found" Whiskey in Your Craft Distillery

Casey Miles

Here is how to take a 53-gallon barrel of "new make" whiskey and make 1,243 bottles of rum and whiskey.

In 6–12 months of aging, a $6,000 investment can return $22,000... if you sell 25% of the bottles from your retail location for $35 each and 75% of the bottles through distribution for $12.50 each.

STEP 1

Buy a 53-gallon barrel of whiskey from a big distillery (a pallet is four barrels and should run less than $3,000). A barrel of unaged corn whiskey should run $700. (www.mgpigredients.com)

STEP 2

Dump the barrel of new whiskey into your 53-gallon still. Make a run and cut 5% as heads. Shut off the still and pump the whiskey out through a heat exchanger. Proof to 128 (64% ABV).

STEP 3

Buy 15-gallon (char level 3) barrels and fill with redistilled whiskey.

STEP 4

Buy a 55-gallon drum of molasses and make rum. This rum is backfilled into the empty whiskey barrel.

STEP 5

Age both the whiskey and the rum for 6–12 months.

STEP 6

Marketing. Great labels sell products. Now sell it.

Make vodka in the downtime. Bottle in 750-ml bottles and sell for $25 each.

Double the rum output and bottle half as a white rum as well. Sell at $25 each.

In states where it is legal, you can make ready-to-drink cocktails in a bottle and easily sell 750-ml bottles for $15 each.

Sell cocktails in your tasting room (i.e., Mojito, Old Fashioned, Manhattan or just serve neat). $10 per drink is $100 profit per bottle.

This process is not limited to single-runs per month. You can do it 10 times per month. $60k of investment would return $220k of product in six months. The trick will be selling it all. Don't forget to make cool-looking crates for merchandise displays at retailers. A 1' x 8' cedar fence board for $3 can be stripped, cut and sanded to make really cool-looking crates. Fill them with the straw filler from Uline for a cool look filled with all your 375-ml hip-flask bottles with wax tops!

Tenth Ward Distilling Co.

58 Gin

Admiralty Distillery

Anvil Distillery

Bauernhofbrennerei Luethy

Big Cypress Distillery

Brothers Spirits

Captive Spirits

Coastal Spirits/Farallon Gin Works

Corsair Distillery

Cultus Bay Distillery

Doc Herson's Natural Spirits

Dominion Distillery

Eaglesburn Distillery

Ermest Scarano Distillery

Flying Buck Distillery

Hamilton Distillers

Hartfield & Co.

Heritage Distilling Co.

Hotel Tango Artisan Distillery

Independent Distilling

Ironclad Distilling

Irons Distillery

Kings County Distilling

Lee Spirits

Lyon Distilling

Maiden Distillery

Old Ballard Distillery & Cafe

Old Home Distillers

Rowhouse Spirits

Shady Knoll Farm Distillery

Sheringham Distillery

Standard Spirits

Whiskey Gap Distillery

Part Four
Nano Distillery Profiles

Mark Marmont
Hackney Downs Studios
3017 Amhurst Terrace
London, E8 2BT UK

Carmen@58gin.com
58gin.com

Products: Gin Original, Limited Edition and the Chocolate Negroni have won numerous awards

Backstory: The 58 Gin story began when Mark Marmont moved to London from Australia. But it wasn't until settling near to The Bar With No Name that Mark discovered what would become his true passion. Mark became a frequent visitor to the bar, sampling the multiple gin-based cocktails on offer. Before long, Mark was fully immersed in investigation of the distillation process and exploring how gin was made. Yet he couldn't find a gin that he liked. In the couple of experimental years that followed, Mark became affectionately known as "Moonshine Mark" by the regulars at the bar. It was during this time that he perfected his recipe and 58 Gin was born, named after Mark's house number. His distilling equipment was made by Al-Ambiq in Portugal. Classes in making gin are offered at the distillery.

Admiralty Distillery

Owner, Distiller: Jake Soule
820 Lake St.
Port Townsend, WA 98368
(360) 643-3530

jsourle1@gmail.com
admiraltydistillers.com

Number of Employees: Himself

Annual Production: (9-L cases): 2,000 bottles

% of Production Sold In-house
(Tasting Room): 90%

Still Manufacturer and Size: 150-gallon
Adrian Edelbrände

Products: Fruit brandy (apples and pears), marc brandy styled after classic Italian grappa, using pressed grapes, grape skins, seeds, a small quantity of pulp, must and wine. The spirits rest for one year before bottling at 42–45% ABV. Brandy is distilled from Orange Muscat grapes (*Vitis vinifera* species) and with other Washington-grown varietals.

Pennant Gin, originally hoisted in the 1940s as an invitation from one naval ship to another for officers to come aboard for a ration of gin. Grapes are used for the base of this gin.

Distilling: An eau de vie (French for "water of life") is a clear, colorless fruit brandy created by means of careful fermentation and distillation. The fruit flavor is typically very light. Ripe fruit is fermented, distilled and quickly bottled to preserve the freshness of the parent fruit. Eaux de vie are typically not aged in wood casks, hence they are clear, although some of our products are barrel-aged.

Tours upon request and we will never pass your email address around!

As a young man, Jake was drawn to spirits over beer. Later in life, looking for a profession that would hold his interest and offer excitement, artistry, chemistry and a little voodoo, he settled on craft distilling.

Admiralty Distillers uses as much local product as possible. The rye comes from Finn River Farm, a small farm just seven miles from the distillery. The signature marc brandy is produced from Marechal Foch grapes grown nearby on a friend's acreage, just three miles away. And in the fall, apples are gleaned from in-town locals whose trees have overproduced. "I get apples from wherever I can."

Finally: Do you still have your day job?
(x) Yes ( ) No

Jake works as a carpenter.

Peter & Christa Grundy, Founders
Dean Marraccini, Distiller
117 S. Sunset St. Ste. G1
Longmont, CO 80501
(720) 600-5103

peter@anvildistillery.com
anvildistillery.com

Check website for free tours, tasting room and cocktail hours!

Videos: Youtube.com/watch?v=jPsCSNo8wZQ

Products: All are distilled from scratch. Grumpy's Vodka, Ironface Gin, whiskey and rum are also in production.

Equipment: Electric 26- and 100-gallon Hillbilly stills. We also use a 120-gallon Bubba's Barrels mash tun with false bottom to cook grains and have several Bubba's Barrels conical fermentation tanks.

Production: Approximately 500 to 600 bottles a month. 50% sold in CO under our self-distribution wholesale license. The other 50% sold at our tasting room in Longmont.

Check our website to find locations that sell our products within CO.

We also just started with a distributor for NY and NJ.

Backstory: We currently sell through everything we distill every month and are planning to expand operations. We selected the name Anvil Distillery because it very clearly symbolizes the notion of hand-crafted through skill and hard work.

As a nano distillery, we are proud to say everything we produce is hand-crafted.

Finally: Do you still have your day job?
Yes (x) No ( )

[Peter's answer]:I do but my wife and father-in-law, Dean, run things during the day.

Bauernhofbrennerei Lüthy

Urs Luethy, Owner/Distiller
Suhrgasse 27
5037 Muhen, Switzerland
+ 41-62-7231169

info@brennerei-luethy.ch
www.brennerei-luethy.ch

Open Friday and Saturday for tastings and sales, or by appointment.

Equipment: One trailer (Stoerbrennerei) with two 20-gallon pot stills, made more than 100 years ago by the former Gleis company in Switzerland, fired directly with wood.

Four 39-gallon Holstein pot stills with three-layer copper columns each, gas-heated, mostly used for contract distilling.

Production: (2016): About 500 gallons, 50% sold at the distillery and 50% in local stores and at events.

Products: Eaux de vie: cherry, apple, pear, quince, damson, potato (Haerdoepfeler). Whiskey: Swiss single malt (Herr Luethy) and Swiss spelt whisky (Seetaler Ur-Dinkel), absinthe.

Backstory: Urs Luethy's father started the spirits business in 1997, concentrating mostly on contract distilling for farmers in the region. When his son, who had a particular liking for Scotch, entered the business, it didn't take long until he made his first whiskey in 2005. For this, he purchased and carefully renovated a very old "Stoerbrennerei," a mobile distilling system with a long tradition in Switzerland.

With this cart, originally pulled by horses, he joined whiskey events all over Switzerland and distilled in public. Once, the cart of 4,000 lbs. was even lifted to the top of the Titlis Mountain by a helicopter in order to make whiskey at an altitude of 9,900 ft.

Urs Luethy puts a lot of emphasis on producing whiskey of purely Swiss origin. Therefore, having built a malting floor adjoining his distillery, he started malting the barley grown on his own farmland. Even the aging process takes place in barrels made from Swiss oak. There is no other distiller in Switzerland who follows the rules of "pure Swissness" so strictly.

13995 SW 144th Ave. #207
Miami, FL 33186
(786) 228-9740

bigcypressdistillery.com

Products: Specializing in the production of fine American whiskey, American gin and rum

Backstory: Big Cypress Distillery is a family affair. Cousins Fernando and Mark and in-law Danny founded the distillery in 2015 from a shared passion for American craft whiskey, craft rum and south Florida artistry. Head Distiller Fernando Plata served with the 82nd Airborne and spent 20 years as a software professional. He respects American distilling traditions, believes in innovation and is a stickler for quality.

The name Big Cypress derives from an appreciation for the outdoors and an affinity for Everglades backcountry fishing. It's an homage to where we're from. In crafting our fine spirits, we source ingredients from local vendors, never compromise on quality, strive for innovation while respecting the tradition of American distilling and believe in being transparent about our ingredients and process.

We have to thank the gang at M.I.A. Beer company (Miami) for making this collaboration a reality. They make an awesome gruit. We hope that the love we have for where we're from comes through in our craft spirits.

Brothers Spirits

Jeff & Jay Lockwood, Owner/Distillers
201 Industrial Way, Unit D
Buelton, CA 93427
(805) 691-9259

www.brothersspirits.com

Products: Spirits Vodka, Blanco Agave Azul, Tegave, White Hawk Malt Whiskey and limoncello

Equipment: Our still was made by Mile Hi Distilling of Denver. It's a 53-gallon pot with a six-section, six-inch column, heated with two 5,500-watt coils. The still makes great products, and we have no complaints.

Being a nano distillery, we need to cut costs as much as possible, so to save money I made a silk-screen box and do all our bottle labeling by hand. I also rigged a set-up to do my own zesting of our lemons and oranges. It's all about Redneck Engineering 101 here. Our fermentation vessels are 55-gallon HDPE barrels with a waterbed heater and thin aluminum insulation wrapped around each barrel. The system works and we're in business for little money.

Backstory: Everyone knows about California wines being the best in the world. So why not make a vodka/neutral brandy out of the finest wine grapes in the world? That is exactly what Brothers Spirits does. We can ship our product within California as long as it is called neutral brandy.

Brothers Blanco Agave Azul—Made in America with the soul of Mexico. Because it's not made in Mexico, we call our 100% agave spirit "Agave Azul." We use 100% certified organic-grown Agave tequilana (blue agave) grown in Jalisco, Mexico, in a little town called Villa Corona, southwest of Guadalajara, where they harvest, cook and squeeze the piñas to produce the juice that is sent to us. We ferment and then distill it three times. One sip and you will not want to buy any other brand.

Our White Hawk Single Malt Whiskey contains fresh malted barley, with peated and mesquite-smoked barley added to the mash. We use the right temperature to create a whiskey wash for fermentation and distillation.

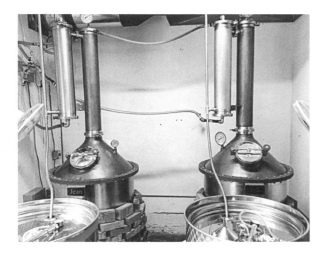

Ben Capdevielle, Distiller & co-owner
with Holly Robinson, Todd Leabman &
Erica Goodkind
41518 NW 52nd St.
Seattle, WA 98107
(206) 852-4794

Holly@captivespiritsdistilling.com
captivespiritsdistilling.com
facebook.com/CaptiveSpiritsBigGin

Please call for tour appointments.

Equipment: 2 x 100-gallon Vendome. A third still will be added at a new facility. The stills are all named after our departed grandmothers, Phyllis, Jean and Bobbi.

Number of Employees: 3 plus Hood River Distillers' distribution/sales team

Annual Production: 7,000 cases. 1% of production sold in-house (tasting room)

Products: Big Gin and Bourbon Barrel Aged Big Gin

Backstory: Opened in 2010. A third-generation distiller (his granddad and dad are moonshiners), Ben believes in creating a product ginners can recognize: a crisp, London Dry Gin. "No flowers or cucumbers were ever harmed in the making of Big Gin."

Welcome to Captive Spirits Distilling, where we make Big Gin and various barreled renditions in the Ballard neighborhood of Seattle. Family-run, we are exclusively a gin company, focused on making only gin in a traditionally distilled manner. Loads of juniper, bitter orange peel and Tasmanian pepperberries help create a bold gin. Yes, we like the taste of juniper. Yes, we love gin. Knock on our door if you're in the neighborhood, or walk back into our side alley, where you'll often find us distilling with the garage doors open.

Coastal Spirits/Farallon Gin Works

Brad Plummer Owner/Distiller
110 Glenn Way #2
San Carlos, CA 94070
(650) 232-7331

brad@ginfarallon.com
coastalspirits.co

Tours by appointment.

Distribution: California, Epic Wines and Spirits

Equipment: 53-gallon, electric Mile Hi hybrid still—four-inch column with four plates and dephlegmator. Column used as botanical basket when plates are out.

Products: Gin Farallon, 43% ABV; Vodka Farallon, 40% ABV; plus numerous private-label contract products.

Production: 500 9-L cases per year

Backstory: I had been dabbling with brewing beer and winemaking at home, when I caught the gin bug. It turned out to be a lot harder to make than I'd imagined. In 2012, my wife and I decided to open a distillery with the goal of focusing on crafting a truly "California" gin. I built a small 15-gallon pilot still to begin formulating gin recipes, and I left my job at Stanford University in early 2014 to work on Coastal Spirits full time. We launched our first product, Vodka Farallon, in the fall of 2014.

This year (2017) we are expanding our team and re-branding the distillery as "Farallon Gin Works." Named after the iconic island chain 30 miles off the coast of San Francisco, "farallon" means "sea cliff" Spanish. My gin and vodka were developed in partnership with my local water district on the California coast, where I draw raw spring water from the cliffs overlooking the Pacific. On a clear day, you can see the Farallon Islands from the well I use.

Currently I re-distill NGS using a 53-gallon hybrid electric still from Mile Hi Distilling. In September 2017, we ordered a much larger 600-L steam-fired pot still with a gin basket and six-plate side column (made by Daeyoo Tech, China), to be installed in Spring 2018.

I quit my day job in 2014, but I continue to work as a freelance writer and editor on the side.

Darek Bell Owner/Distiller
Andrew Webber/Distiller
601 Merritt Ave.
Nashville, TN 37203
(615) 200-0320

darek@corsairartisan.com
www.corsairartisan.com

Second location, Nashville-Merritt Ave.-
Wedgewood Houston
Corsair Distillery and Taproom
1200 Clinton St. #110
Nashville, TN 37203
(270) 904-2021

Custom-made pot stills and libation bar where you can taste the full Corsair spirits lineup. We also offer craft cocktail flights. We offer rare distiller-selected single-barrel bottling.
-Nashville-Clinton St.-Marathon Village Corsair Brewstillery

You might ask yourself, "What's a brewstillery? Is it a brewery? Is it a distillery?" The answer is both. At our original Nashville location, we have expanded our focus to include high-gravity beer with our malt-whiskey program.

Kentucky Corsair Distillery
400 E. Main Ave. #110
Blowing Green, KY 42101
(270) 904-2021

Our original distillery is located in downtown Bowling Green, Kentucky. At this location, we offer tours of the distillery where we make our unique gin, vodka and absinthe. You can make an appointment to take a science-based walk through the distillery and do a botanical-forward tour of gin and whiskey being made. In the tasting room, we offer the full Corsair spirits lineup. The original still (pictured) in Bowling Green is a 50-gallon pot still. It was manufactured by Vendome, in Louisville, KY.

The online gift shop offers the award-winning book ALT WHISKEY and 15 gal. used/empty oak barrels. Corsair also operates its own malthouse, where they smoke wheat, hickory, applewood and pecan (available from the website).

Products—Current Releases: Artisan gin, red absinthe, vanilla bean spiced rum, triple smoke quinoa whiskey and Ryemageddon.

We have 19 seasonal products available.

Awards
2015 Innovator of the Year, Fast Company Magazine
2014 Innovator of the Year, Whiskey Magazine
2014 Distillery of the Year, American Distilling Institute
2014 American Craft Distiller of the Year, Wizards of Whisky
2013 Craft Whiskey of the Year, Whiskey Advocate

Cultus Bay Distillery

Kathy Parks, Distiller
Harry Sloan, Partner
8311 Sandy Hook Drive
Clinton, WA 98236

For a tour, contact kathyparks@shidbey.com

A nano fermenting wash and distilling gin, vodka and whiskey

Self-Distributed

Equipment: The distillery is built from equipment found on eBay.

Backstory: Opening in 2016, this nano is very, very small—just 288 sq. ft.—and located in a converted boathouse. The distillery is just steps away from the dock with its sacks of oysters swaying happily in the Puget Sound waters. Kathy Parks (73) and her partner, Harry Sloane lll, are distilling three distinctive products: Mortal Gin, Te Absolvo Vodka (they are both Catholics) and a traditional Irish poitin. Kathy points out that when she started the distillery, she could barely lift 20 pounds; now she is easily moving around 40-pound bags of grain. With her extensive artistic background, she designed the product labels and leaves a lot of the math and distillery paperwork to Harry. "If I had known there was so much math involved, I might not have been so interested!"

Harry is a substance abuse counselor, Kathy works the distillery.

Kevin Herson & Stacy Luckow, Founders
630 Flushing Ave
Brooklyn, NY 11206
917-370-1216

info@dochersons.com
dochersons.com

Tour by Appointment

National Distribution. Projected annual sales 500 9L cases.

Equipment: 53 gallon Still Dragon Still

Backstory: Founded in a Harlem basement, 380 sq ft, (2012) Doc Herson's Natural Spirits is the first absinthe distillery in New York City. Growing up in South Africa, master distiller Kevin Herson, formulated concoctions with his now antique chemistry set. His love for culture led him to travel the world and experience food and drinks of all customs and varieties. With a doctorate degree, "The Doc" has developed a unique palate for distilling spirits, introducing exemplary palliative delights to the world of craft spirits.

We start by fermenting malted barley and malted spelt, organic grains from upstate New York. We ferment with sugar, yeast and New York tap water. The wash is then run through a column still to produce 50% raw spirit, then 10 different dried botanicals from around the world are added and left to steep for one week. Herbs include grand wormwood, anise, fennel, dried lemons, mint and others as part of our secret recipe. After the week of steeping, the raw spirit along with the herbs are then thrown in to our pot still and fractionally distilled off to collect the hearts and portions of the tails containing the herbaceous oils and flavors. Once the fractional distillation is complete, the spirit is diluted down to 66% using New York tap water, additional herbs including fresh mint leaves for our Green Absinthe and whole dried hibiscus flowers for our Red Absinthe are then added to color and flavor the absinthe. Lastly the spirit is strained from the herbs, bottled, wax sealed and hand labeled, each bottle individually, all done by us.

Kevin Herson of Doc Herson's Natural Spirits is located in a former Pfizer laboratory building in Brooklyn, and only a few yards away from another nano distillery, Standard Spirits.
Photo © Andrew Faulkner

Green Absinthe Tasting Notes: A complex yet delicate balance of botanicals. Subtle wormwood on the nose with hints of anise and fresh mint. Sharp on the palate with sweet licorice countering the bitter wormwood. A bright citrus-full mouth feel, slightly dry yet complex. Refreshing and soothing herbal finish.

Made with organic grains from upstate New York and 11 different botanicals, our Green Absinthe made entirely in house from fermentation to bottle, can be enjoyed simply over ice or in any of the various traditional cocktails prepared with Absinthe. Or one can simply enjoy it as a cocktail with ice, seltzer and a squeeze of lemon.

Red Absinthe Tasting Notes: A complex yet delicate balance of botanicals. Subtle anise on the nose with hints of wormwood, hibiscus and lemon citrus. Soft on the palate with sweet hibiscus countering the bitter wormwood. A bright citrus-full mouth feel, slightly dry yet complex. Refreshing and soothing floral finish.

Made with organic grains from upstate New York and 11 different botanicals, our Red Absinthe made entirely in house from fermentation to bottle, can be enjoyed simply over ice or in any of the various traditional cocktails prepared with absinthe. Or one can simply enjoy it as a cocktail with ice, ginger ale and a squeeze of orange.

Dominion Distillery

Carl "Henry" Anderson
116 N. Main St.
Colville, WA 99114
(509) 675-4794

Henry@dominiondistillery.com
dominiondistillery.com

Products: Single Malt Vodka and
Apple Moonshine

Backstory: Henry is also the owner of Gatling Still
Works, a designer and fabricator of nano craft-
distilling systems. gatlingstillworks.com

"We are ultimately in the flavor business, and
there is only one way to find out what flavor
a new shape of the column will produce and
how it effects certain mash bills." We build very
durable and efficient base kettles with a variety
of interchangeable domes and columns. The
Dominion Distillery is our guinea pig for new
still designs.

We have just released a bain-marie distillery
(double boiler).

Bart Johnson, Owner
Kloosterstraat 15
Netherlands 6981CC
31 641819110

info@eaglesburndistillery.com
eaglesburndistillery.com

Annual Production: 80 (9-L cases) of Eaglesburn Gin. 10% of production is sold in-house at our tasting room. Some international sales.

Backstory: At the age of 22, I was a cameraman for a short film. The director couldn't pay me, but became a good friend. Then on my 23rd birthday, he gave me a bottle of quarter-cask Laphroaig (which I sold). This was my beginning with a long affair with whiskey. In 2014, I started my distillery using a 50-L iStill system. In 2016, I won a gold medal at the Global Spirits Masters competition with my dry gin. Eaglesburn distillery is like most small nano distilleries. I use NGS as a base, then redistill it with a gin basket to produce an award-winning gin. I still have my day job and soon hope to be a full-time distiller.

Ernest Scarano Distillery

Ernest Scarano, Owner/Distiller
4487 Hayes Ave. (S.R. 6)
(419) 205-8734
Fremont, OH 43420

ernie@esdistillery.com
esdistillery.com
Facebook @ErnestScaranodistillery

Tours by appointment one week in advance.

Everything is done at the distillery, from mashing to distilling, aging, bottling, labeling and selling. Ohio is a control state with the Division of Liquor Control regulating prices and bottle size. We accept cash or check, no credit cards. Our products cannot be purchased in liquor stores, only at the distillery. So call and come visit us.

Products: Old Homicide. "It's to die for." It's 140-proof Straight Bonded Whiskey: 375 ml, aged 4 years. $95. Very limited supply. Widmer Winter Rye: $37 for 375 ml, 90 proof.

Equipment: 60-gallon Georgia Ridge still, churns out 150-proof 'shine.

Backstory: A bronze plaque on the distillery wall honors Ernest Scarano, 1919–1988, who served his country during the Second World War, most notably in Operation Torch (November 8–16, 1942), landing with the western task force at Casablanca. The distillery is named in his honor.

"I know that it is not fashionable these days to say kind words about the government, but the Alcohol, Tobacco Tax & Trade Bureau (TTB) is the best-run agency I've ever had to deal with, especially the National Revenue Center in Cincinnati, Ohio. Believe it or not, my permit was given personalized attention by the new permit department and I had everything in place in little over 90 days. Finally, we are proud to be a member of the ADI."

Calvin Riggleman, Owner, Distiller
13841 Northwestern Pike
Augusta, WV 26704
(540) 550-8450

Website: Under construction

Tours. Open daily, tours by appointment

Products: Moonshine, Naughty Oak Spirits Whiskey and Apple Pie Moonshine made from corn grown on the farm. We will also make vodka for fruit cordials from apples, cherries, and raspberries grown in our orchards.

Equipment: Electric 200-liter (53-gal.) reflux from Mile Hi

Projected annual production: 500 9-L cases. 70% to be sold to West Virginia and Virginia ADC, 30% at tasting room. Come by and see us.

Backstory: Flying Buck is located in a 1960s milking barn on Brigg Riggs Farm. The barn sits on a short dirt road just off Route 50. Some GPS services can't find us, so call if you get lost. Look for an American flag on the side of the barn.

Hamilton Distillers

Stephen Paul, Founder
2106 North Forbes Blvd #103
Tuscon, AZ 85745
(520) 628-628

i nfo@hamiltondistillersy.com
hamiltondistillers.com

Products: Dorado, Mesquite Smoked Aged (Single Malt). Clear-Mesquite Smoked Unaged (90 proof). Classic, is unsmoked and aged (84 proof). Classic with caramel, molasses and marzipan on the nose, and ripe stone fruits up front on the palate, delivers a spice and honey finish. After pouring, let it rest in the glass for a few minutes and nose before tasting.

Events: We are opening up our space to the public for Second Saturdays. Our open hours will be 4 pm to 8 pm. We will be selling whiskey by the glass and flights until close. There is live music, corn hole, chess and cards. No sign-up required—come one, come all.

Backstory: After years of crafting furniture that was authentic, lasting and handmade (in-house kiln-dried wood), we decided that Hamilton's whiskeys would also be handmade. We would malt our own barley; mash, ferment, distill, barrel and bottle under one roof. We would be proud to say we do it all ourselves.

Hamilton Spirits began in 2011, when we purchased a 50-gallon Hoga pot still from Portugal, what we call today a nano still. This small still was a way to get started. We needed to learn the process of distilling whiskey. We also had to learn how to malt barley. At first, we were using 6-row cattle-feed barley from nearby Collidge, AZ, and later 2-row distiller malt. We took the process one more step and smoked our barley over mesquite wood. This gives us a "smoked single-malt flavor" distinctive to the American Southwest.

By January of 2014, enough investment had been raised to begin implementing a 500-gallon distilling system and we were soon aging barrels of whiskey. In the early years, we floor-malted 70-lb. batches. Our new malthouse allows us to make 5,000-lb, batches using a two-tank system in which we are able to steep, germinate and dry. This system gives us more control, resulting in better malt. You can taste the difference.

Above—Smoked grains make an important contribution to the flavor profile of Haminlton Distillers' Whiskey Del Bac, Stephen Paul, founder of Hamilton Distillers. Photo © Steven Meckler.

Left— Stephen Paul, founder of Hamilton Distillers. Photo © Steven Meckler.

Andrew & Larissa Buchanan
718 Main St.
Paris, KY 40361
(859) 559-3494

infor@hartfieldandcompany.com
hartfieldandcompany.com

The first new distillery in Bourbon County since 1919.

Products: For our mainline bourbon, we use 19% rye, 19% malted barley and 62% corn. We have taken the malted barley from merely an engine for the starch conversion and moved it more into the territory of a flavor grain. That starts to add more flavors like smoke and tobacco notes to our bourbon. We get a lot of comparisons to having something with a Scotch-type flavor combined with a more traditional bourbon profile.

Most bourbon is distilled at or just below 160 proof, the legal upper distillation limit for bourbons and whiskeys. At that level, you are only 40 proof from pure alcohol and 30 proof from being able to call it vodka. Eighty percent alcohol is what you have. Which means you only have 20 percent left for any flavor. Legal barrel entry for bourbon is 125 proof. If you are distilling at or just below 160 proof, whatever you have just distilled (thus whatever flavor profile) is cut before it goes into the barrel.

We treat our distillation a lot more like brandy. Our stills are column-reflux batch stills, so we shoot for an overall proof of somewhere between 115–120 proof. We distill a bit further down into the proof ranges, which brings up some oil from the grain with the distillate. This is what gives our bourbon a very full mouthfeel that lasts and lasts.

Again, we like a lot of the bourbons that are produced in this manner. There are some amazing bourbons in the world that started their existence just like this. We have chosen to do it differently in hope of retaining more flavor.

Equipment: Our stills come from Hillbilly Stills in Barlow, KY. Two 26-gallon stills with an all-copper 100-gallon still. We had them custom-build the columns with our distillation technique in mind. There are two plate columns rather than the traditional four, leaving us with the ability to leave flavor in rather than stripping so much out in the first run. We use the same configuration for both whiskeys and rums, with the focus on flavor retention.

Backstory: The law in Kentucky was changed at the beginning of 2016, going into effect in July. It allows us to have a full NQ3 license, which in Kentucky is a full-bar license. This is a game changer for distilleries our size, allowing for a completely different revenue stream. For some of the big distilleries, this change might make their visitor center a little more lively, but in reality would be just a blip in their financial report. For us, it could be huge. We are approaching it with curation and education in mind. Exposing our customers to new brands that we feel comfortable getting behind, telling their story and sharing the liquid which they worked so hard to produce. The great folks at the Kentucky Distillers' Association spearheaded the change in legislation, with everyone understanding what kind of an impact this can have.

Everything we distill goes directly into our barrels. All of the flavor from all of the grains that we work so hard to move around isn't cut before we hit that barrel. More than anything, we want the grains that we are using to be represented in the final flavor profile. If we change the mashbill a few percentage points or substitute malted rye for traditional rye, we want to be able to taste that change. This goal is achieved by not distilling to such a high proof, which strips the flavor out of the distillate. We currently age in 5.8-gallon barrels from The Barrel Mill in Minnesota. These are all American white oak and char #3. That first bit is required by law. Our mainline bourbon ages between 3.5–4.5 months, all depending on the barrel. Some barrels take a bit longer to hit their peak.

We taste our barrels starting around 3 months. This gives us a great look at the progression of the flavor profile, and means we end up tasting a lot of bourbon. Tough job. It allows us to hone in on the flavor profile that we are trying to achieve. Hartfield continues page 116

Each barrel is different, which is common. Taste through barrel samples at big distilleries and you will see the same. As controlled as we keep everything throughout the distillation process, we leave the final stage up to nature. We, as an industry, leave the final development of our beloved product up to what the wood will do to the spirits we put inside them.

The last step on the journey to the bottle is blending. Using small barrels can sometimes mean the flavor profile of that barrel is pretty skewed. Some barrels can really have lots of caramel and a smooth finish, but nothing else. Some barrels can taste perfect, but not possess a good mouthfeel. It is up to us to blend these barrels together to match our intended profile. Each batch usually has 6–9 barrels in it, yielding between 180–280 bottles (750 ml).

Once we have tasted and all agree on the blend, we get to bottling.

Justin Stiefel Owner & Distiller

3207 57th St. Ct. NW
Gig Harbor WA 98335

Capitol Hill Tasting Room
1201 10th Ave.
Seattle, WA 98122

Eugene, OR Tasting Room
110 Madison St.
Eugene, OR 97402

heritagedistilling.com
www.facebook.com/heritagedistilling/

Products: The Cask Club lineup at the tasting rooms at Capitol Hill and Eugene, OR, have a full range of products that include whiskey, gin and vodkas. Offering 24 naturally flavored vodkas, bourbon, rye, blended whiskey, gin and vodka. Flavored whiskeys. Samples, mini-cocktails and bottle sales to go, plus a full range of merchandise and gifts.

Equipment: At Heritage Distillery we have a 3,000-L, 14-foot, 12-plate combo still and a continuous polishing column, 20-feet tall with 32 plates. On location we mash, ferment and distill for both tasting rooms.

Capital Hill Tasting Room—Five 26-gallon Hillbilly stills with the wash coming from Heritage Distillery in Gig Harbor. The stills will be upgraded to 100 gallons in 2017.

Eugene, OR Tasting Room—Six Hillbilly stills and a 50-gallon StillDragon set-up. The equipment will be upgraded to 100-gallon stills in the spring. All wash is currently coming from Heritage Distillery in Eugene.

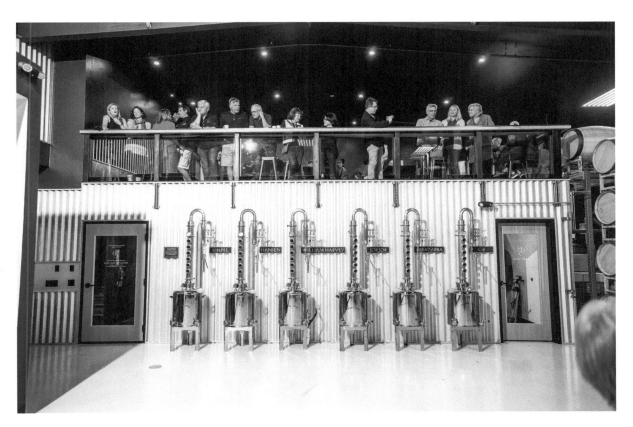

Hotel Tango Artisan Distillery

Travis Barnes
702 Virginia Ave.
Indianapolis, IN 46203
(317) 653-1806

infor@hoteltangowhiskey.com
hoteltangowhiskey.com

Backstory: The founder of Hotel Tango, Travis Barnes, fought for our country with great pride in three combat tours in Iraq, making Hotel Tango a one-of-a-kind destination place in Indy.

Comments from Customers: Well, just give me a shot, sit me by the fireplace and let me snuggle that crazy cat all day long!

Top 5 favorites about Hotel Tango:

1. The cozy vibe right when you walk in the door.

2. The crackling of the fireplace, making you feel like you're tucked away in a log cabin in the woods.

3. The friendly faces at the bar—the bartenders are great! Not sure what you want? Let them know what you like, and they'll give you great recommendations.

4. Complimentary popcorn—well, this just couldn't get any better! My favorite snack right at the tip of my fingers... and free!

5. Hot spiced rum. This drink just gives me all the feels on these cold, wintery days.

Michael Anderson, Owner/Distiller
731 E. College Ave.
Decatur, GA 30030
(678) 576-3804

Tours: Saturday 2 pm–5 pm

Backstory: Our first product was Hellbender Corn Whiskey. It is made from locally sourced (non-GMO) corn from Riverview Farms in Ranger, GA. The mashbill is 83% corn and 17% malted barley. It is designed to be a full-flavored whiskey with a big corn punch. (Corn whiskey is a southern tradition that has been lost by mainstream spirits producers.) Our Hellbender Bourbon is aged in new charred American white oak barrels for an average of 15 months. Each batch is distinct, with slight variations from the wood contribution. The bourbon has a great depth of oak and vanilla on the nose that translates on the palate with hints of corn and burnt orange, finishing with rich baking spices.

Our third product is Independent Rum, made from table-grade molasses that is long-fermented and lightly distilled to create a distinctive full flavor.

We just did a collaboration with Three Taverns Brewery to create Georgia's first bierschnaps as part of our Outlier series, which has a limited release. It is made with Three Tavern's 100% malted barley Feest Noel (merriment in a glass) and also contains Belgian dark candy sugar, along with cardamom, allspice and cloves that carry on in the distillation process. Our stills are a 100-gallon Hoga from Spain and a 500-gallon Corsan hybrid. Take home a bottle.

(And: Yes, I still have a day job.)

Ironclad Distillery

Stephen King, Owner
Owen King, Distiller
124 23rd St.
Newport News, VA 23607
(757) 245-1996

ironcladdistillery.com
soundcloud.com/qaapc/
episode-18-ironclad-distillery-co

Products: Ironclad Bourbon is currently available in select Virginia and D.C. stores. Ironclad can also be ordered online at adb.virginia.gov.

Equipment: We do our stripping runs in five 26-gallon boilers and collect 25 gallons. This is transferred to the column still (also 26 gallons) where it receives its second distillation. The end result is 160-proof heaven!

"Oak Is Ironclad": Virginia oak barrels give bourbon 100% of its color and 70% of its flavor over months and years. But after it's finished refining bourbon, a barrel is never finished.

On our website, you can register your barrel with a BarrelTag, allowing you to follow a barrel's afterlife. So, if one day it ends up aging local beer or honey, or it becomes a funky piece of furniture, you can track the life of the barrel.

Backstory: Ironclad Bourbon is made from local Virginia corn, wheat and rye, along with malted barley. It is aged in new American oak (charred) barrels. It is characterized by the brackish air from Virginia's James River, balanced with the sweet caramelized oak sap from small barrels. Each batch is double-distilled in six 26-gallon stainless steel stills and generally aged over two summers. The result? A sweet opening and a dry spice pop that's ideal in a glass on its own and works great in cocktails.

The distillery is located inside the Paul David Building, directly across the street from Newport News City Hall.

Jeffrey Irons, Owner/Distiller
2251 Governors Bend Rd.
Huntsville, AL 35801
(256) 536-0100

Ironsonewhiskey@gmail.com
Ironsone.com

Products: Bourbon Mash Whiskey and Bourbon Whiskey. Come by for a tour and a tasting.

Backstory: My relationship with whiskey began when I was 18 years old. I grew up in New Jersey and had a tight group of good high-school friends. We loved to go to bars in Greenwood Lake, New York, which was a 45-minute drive. And the reason we drove to New York to go to bars is simple. New York had a drinking age of 18, while New Jersey was 21. We went to Greenwood Lake, a New York City summertime bedroom community, that was surrounded by bars that catered to the young NJ drinking crowd who routinely drove across state lines to imbibe their favorite alcoholic beverage. The only problem we had was the high cost of the cover charge and the cost of drinks, both of which were extreme compared to high-school wages (mine came from being a busboy at the Lake Mohawk Country Club and delivering flowers for Redshaw's Florist). We had to watch our consumption rate due to the NY and NJ police that were keeping close tabs on us barely legal drinkers.

We always had a pact to pick a designated driver—who, although we didn't require not to drink, had to drink much less than the others crammed into the car. More often than not, I was the DD since I was trying to be responsible. So, I would limit myself to one drink. And I chose to drink whiskey—neat.

Distillation: Once the alcohol starts to flow out of the still, I taste the product, and when it starts taking on a sweet taste and corn aroma, I start collecting the "hearts." The hearts are the distillate that I age in charred oak barrels.

The hearts flow for the longest part of the distilling process. At the end of the hearts, the head temperature begins to creep up, an indication that my run is nearing the "tails" phase. The taste of the distillate begins to pick up a lot of flavor. This flavor adds a lot to the final product, but you can't take too much of it because it can ruin the taste of the distilled and aged product with that bitter "moonshine taste."

Kings County Distillery

Colin Spoelman, Founder/Distiller
David Haskell, Co-founder
Brooklyn Navy Yard, Bldg. 121
Brooklyn, NY 11205
(917) 822-7903

info@kingscountydistillery
kingscountydistillery.com
Facebook Kings County Distillery @KingsCoWhiskey

Tours and tastings Tuesday through Sunday afternoons, and the tasting room is open every day.

Products: Moonshine, Bourbon, Chocolate Whiskey, Peated Bourbon, Barrel Strength Bourbon, Winter Spice Whiskey, Bottled-In-Bond Bourbon, Single Malt Whiskey. Four Year Bottled-in-Bond release (single barrels—112 bottles) and our latest release, Jalapeno Grapefruit Moonshine.

Gatehouse open for summer months. A destination for whiskey lovers, with a retail shop, morning coffee, cocktails and flights of Kings County whiskey. In a beautifully restored building and private outdoor garden. Visit the website for cool gifts.

Books: *Guide to Urban Moonshining: How to Make and Drink Whiskey* and *Dead Distillery: A History of the Upstarts and Outlaws Who Make American Sprits*

Backstory: Kings County Distillery is New York City's oldest operating whiskey distillery, the first since Prohibition. Founded in 2010, Kings County makes moonshine, bourbon and other whiskeys in the 117-year-old Paymaster Building in the Brooklyn Navy Yard. The distillery has been praised by the New York Times, Wine & Spirits, GQ and the New Yorker. "We distill our whiskey from scratch and we never buy whiskey from any other source."

First located in a 325-sq. ft. room (see photo) in East Williamsburg, Kings County began as the smallest commercial distillery in the county (a true nano), with five 24-liter (6.3-gallon) stainless steel stills making whiskey seven days a week, 16 hours a day. In 2012, they moved to the Paymaster Building in the Brooklyn Navy Yard. Today, they have three state-of-the-art (see photo) Forsyth (Scottish) stills and five employees. They do traditional double-distilling and fermentation in wooden fermenters. They purchase corn and barley from small New York State farms. The distillery is a model of sustainable and traditional whiskey production. Kings County was awarded ADI's prestigious Bubble Cap Award for Distillery of the Year in 2016.

Far left—Distiller Garvin James feeds grain into the Vendome cooker while making whiskey at Kings County Distilling.
Left—Flasks of Whiskey line the shelves in the gift shop at Kings County Distillery. This minimalist packaging, reminiscent of a mid-20th century moonshine bottle, has earned design awards and serves as a friendly ambassador for the distillery's spirits.
Photos ©Andrew Faulkner

Nick Lee, Owner
110 E. Boulder St.
Colorado Springs, CO 80905
(719) 659-6213

nick@leespirits.com
leespirits.com
www.facebook.com/LeeSpirits/

Backstory: Lee's is a nano distillery and speakeasy with a focus on gin. Distilling is done in a 50-gallon stainless-steel drum system. They use neutral grain sprits (NGS) as a base, re-distill it to create their gin, dry gin, barrel-aged gin and, most recently released, a lavender spirit. Ninety percent of their spirits are sold in-house as cocktails, and 10% is bottled and distributed to liquor stores, bars and restaurants in the Colorado Springs area.

What makes Lee Spirits a success: Nick makes great martinis, and Lee Spirits is a fun place to hang out.

Check out the short film on the website!

Lyon Distilling Company

Ben Lyon, Jaime Windon, Founders/Distillers
605 South Talbot St. #6
St. Michaels, MD 21663
(443) 333-9131

liquor@lyondistilling.com
lyondistilling.com

Open 7 days a week for tastings and sales, tours on Saturdays or by appointment.

Equipment: Five 26-gallon Hillbilly pot stills with modified 3-inch copper columns. Two 100-gallon mash tuns.

Production (2016): Under 3,000 gallons—60% sold at the distillery, 40% wholesale in Maryland & D.C.

Products: Rum: White Rum, Dark Rum, Sailors Reserve, Overproof White Rum, Overproof French Oak finished Rum. Whiskey: Free State Rye Whiskey, New Make Corn Whiskey, American Malt Whiskey. Liqueur: Curaçao Orange Liqueur, Coffee Rum, Rock & Rum. Many have limited availability due to ultra-small batch size.

Backstory: Lyon Distilling Company is a nano distillery located in St. Michaels, Maryland, steps from the Chesapeake Bay. Founded in 2012, the distillery launched with a signature line of rums paying tribute to the rich, spirited traditions of the Eastern Shore. Hand-crafted from start to finish, Lyon spirits begin as intentionally-sourced raw ingredients and are hand-crafted—mashed, fermented and double-distilled in small pot stills—every step of the way, resulting in a superior and unique product. The goal is to create distinctly American spirits—working to define the category of new American rum and perfecting Maryland Rye Whiskey & American Malt Whiskey, while experimenting with obscure grains and varied finishes.

Helen, Distiller
At the Old Brewery
Maidstone, Kent, UK

info@maidendistillery.com
maidendistillery.com
@Maidendistiller
Facebook/Maidendistillery

Tours: Once a month. Prepaid ticketed events. Open to all 18+

Annual Production: 140 9-L cases, 2% of production sold in-house (tasting room)

Products: Maidstone Gin, using NGS for all products

Equipment: Destilarias Eau de Vie, Iberian Coppers S.A. copper alembic, 100-L

Backstory: I had previous interest in aromatherapy/alchemy and spent several years researching the subject. This led to starting a business making gin and vodka infusions sold in bottles and in cocktails at festivals from my traveling bar ("The Travelling Apothecary"). Interest in local history led to learning about a local distillery in Rochester (Kent). I wanted to learn more about the complete production process and to see if it was possible to add an additional production step to my infusion business, so I visited distilleries in the UK and Europe. Unfortunately, local council did not want a distillery in town and so wouldn't grant permission to use a disused building. This led me to find premises in an adjacent town, which was the best find in the entire story! After further research, I discovered that the proposed premises sat on the same site as an earlier distillery (in production in the early 1800s). The distiller there was the nephew of an extremely well-known distiller, George Bishop, who made Maidstone Geneva, which had several Acts of Parliament passed to protect its production. Copies of original documents were found to prove the provenance. Current tours are conducted to tell others about the original Maidstone Distillery (c. 1770s–March 1817) as well as the other historical distilleries within one mile of Maiden Distillery.

I quit my day job and went full-time at the distillery in September 2016.

Old Ballard Distillery & Cafe

Lexi, Owner
Jane Frazee, Distiller
4421 Shilshole Ave. NW
Seattle, WA 98107
(206) 858-8010

info@oldballardliquorco.com
oldballardliquorco.com
facebook.com/OldBallardLiquorCo

Tours: Call during business hours. Winter hours: October 1–May 31: Sundays, 11 am–7 pm. Closed Monday, Tuesday, Wednesday, and Thursday.

Equipment: 27-gallon Hillbilly still

Production: 223 9-L cases (2,000 liters), 90% of production sold in-house (tasting room).

Distribution: 10% of our vodka is sold to local bars. Self-distribution.

Products: Riktig Aquavit and Cherry Bounce

Backstory: A tiny distillery on the docks in Ballard, creating spirits that keep the Scandinavian heritage of the area alive, including a variety of traditional aquavit. Also a variety of liqueurs created from Pacific Northwest fruit, a "slice of summer in a jar."

This is my full-time day (and night) job.

Aaron Carvell, Distiller/Marketing Director
964 Campbell Rd.
Lebanon, NY 13332
(315)837-4123

office@oldhomedistillers.com
oldhomedistillers.com

Our tasting room is open on Friday, Saturday and Sunday afternoons.

Operations: We operate a family-run New York distillery at our historic property in rural Lebanon, New York, at the geographic heart of the state. We produce small-batch, hand-crafted distilled spirits using locally grown ingredients. We are firmly committed to the creation and successful marketing of high-quality products that will ensure a legacy for our family, benefit local farmers and enrich our corner of Madison County and the State of New York.

Products: Unaged Corn Whiskey (100 proof) is 100% corn. O.H.D. Gin (90 proof) is bold, yet well-mannered. Maple Whiskey (80 proof), a sweet-natured spirit. Applejack (80 proof), has a clear apple character and Spiced (86 proof), our tribute to the flavors of fall. We use the still's gin head to send our whiskey vapors through slices of fresh sweet pumpkin and a special blend of pie-inspired spices. We also offer New York Single Malt Whiskey, Bourbon Whiskey (it's aging) and Field Days Bourbon Whiskey.

Backstory: We opened our doors in less than a year. We submitted our TTB application December 31, 2014, and received it December 19, 2015. And, according to the American Distilling Institute website, anyone who gets their doors open in less than two years will be taken out to dinner by ADI President Bill Owens. (Note: Not many places for dinner in central New York!)

Rowhouse Spirits

Dean Browne Owner/Distiller
2440 Frankford Ave.
Philadelphia, PA 19125
(267) 825-7332

dean@rowhousespirits.up
rowhousespirits.us/

Products: (Our trade secrets are revealed for all to see on our website.)

Poitin: White whiskey, made from 100% malted barley, fermented with beer yeast and run through our small pot still twice. Bottled at 96 proof.

Rowhouse Spirits Gin: Flavored with bright juniper and peppery ginger, with notes of cardamom...ending with citrus and cinnamon from chamomile and cassia bark.

Demon Rum: Made from molasses and panela (sugar), fermented with a funky strain of yeast from the Basque region of Spain. Pot-distilled twice.

Nordic Akvavit: A spirit flavored with caraway, dill and fennel. Aquavit is traditionally taken straight, however, it does make a tasty Bloody Mary.

Bear Trap: An herbal liqueur flavored with 19 distinct herbs and spices. The flavor and aroma of this liqueur is fairly anise-forward with a pleasant herbaceous finish and earthy undertone. Bear Trap, is best enjoyed straight.

Le Coeur Noir: An herbal coffee liqueur made with locally roasted, cold-brewed coffee. Yep, that's what this is. We used fellow Kensington-based, ReAnimator Coffee's Telemetry Blend. ReAnimator roasts and grinds the coffee; we infuse and distill an herbal liquor, cold-brew the coffee and then combine the two. Le Coeur Noir will satisfy even the most black-hearted coffee addict.

Browne Baker Rum: Our friend Tom Baker is best known for his beer. Tom is an owner/brewer of two of Philadelphia's finest brewpubs: Earth Bread + Brewery

photo courtesy of Rowhouse Spirits

and Bar Hygge. What you might not know is that Tom loves his rum. Browne Baker Rum is the result of a collaboration between Dean (me) and Tom. Browne Baker Rum is made in the Jamaican style, using only blackstrap molasses. It is fermented with neutral yeast and then rested in American oak whiskey barrels for six months. The result is a wonderfully sippable rum with almost Scotch-like flavors. Browne Baker Rum is bottled at 90 proof.

Malt Whiskey: Rowhouse Spirits Malt Whiskey is made from 100% malted barley. It is fermented with a special yeast which produces a huge amount of flavor. After being pot-distilled twice, it is rested for a year in American oak barrels which have been used once to age American rye whiskey. The result is a rye-like, full-flavored malt. It is bottled at 100 proof.

Shady Knoll Orchards and Distillery

Richard Kneipper, Distiller
29 Brush Hill Rd.
Millbrook, NY 12545
(214) 850-8409

rick@shadyknolldistillery.com
shadyknolldistillery.com

Equipment: 880-liter (226-gallon) Alambic Charenatais French pot still

Backstory: Shady Knoll historic farm dates back to the 1800s. It is located in the Hudson Valley, near the village of Millbrook, a 1½-hour drive from New York City.

The farm grows its own apples and grains and produces apple brandy and whiskey. The 1,800-acre farm has 87 different varieties of apples, with many varieties recently planted. At the distillery they process, ferment, distill, barrel-age, bottle and label all their products.

Sheringham Distillery (Coastal Craft Spirits)

Jason MacIsaac, Chef turned distiller
Alayne MacIsaac, Entrepreneur & Homesteader,
returning to the island where she grew up
2631 Seaside Dr.
Shirley BC V9Z 1G7
Canada
(778) 528-1313

spirits@sheringhamdistillery.com
sheringhamdistillery.com

Now open Saturdays for tours and tasting, 11 am to 4 pm

Products: Vodka, William's White Double Distilled Grain Spirit, Seaside Gin, Akvavit and launching whiskey in 2018

Akvavit: A traditional Nordic spirit, notes of caraway, anise and citrus with a hint of the ocean from locally harvested winged kelp (Alaria marginata). Made from B.C. organic white wheat, B.C malted barley and botanicals from land and ocean, including sustainable hand-harvested local winged kelp. 42% ABV.

Seaside Gin: Citrus, floral and notes of the sea make our gin as refreshing as a seaside stroll. Elegant for sipping, and noble in your favorite cocktail... clear as the South Island surf. Made from B.C. organic white wheat, B.C. malted barley, natural botanicals and sustainable hand-harvested local winged kelp.

Awards: B.C Distilled 2016 and VISC winner, Gin Category. 43% ABV.

Jason MacIsaac. Photo © David McIlvride

Sasha Selimotic
Taras Hrabowsky
630 Flushing Ave.
Brooklyn, NY 11206

info@ StandardSpirits.com
standardspirits.com

Products: Rye & Corn Heart Cut, Wormwood Rye And Wormwood Gin

Backstory: Our distillery is founded on experimenting with wormwood spirits. Early on, wormwood was an elusive, banned ingredient, but known for its use in traditional absinthe. On our first distillation, we fell in love with more than the myth though—the subtle, lucid, wakeful feel was unlike that of any other spirit. Unknown to us at the time, spirits of wormwood were nearing the end of a century-old ban.

After over a decade of perfecting our unique distilling methods, we are releasing a one-of-a-kind wormwood spirit that departs from traditional absinthe—a wormwood rye. Made from fermenting a rye-and-corn thin mash on the grain, single distilling with a wormwood backset through suspended grains in our modified column still and finally stave-aging with American and French oak. The result is a familiar but new taste of what a rye and wormwood spirit can be. Steering away from traditional herbal absinthe—we don't use anise, licorice or other herbs, just the wormwood—gives the feel of absinthe and the taste of rye.

Tenth Ward Distilling Company

Kyle Pfalzer, Owner
Monica Pearce, Owner
508 E. Church St.
Frederick, MD 21701
(301) 662-4297

www.tenthwarddistilling.com
kylePfalzer@tenthwarddistilling.com, @pfalzerwald
Monica Pearce- monica@tenthwarddistilling.com, @
monquavitae
Verbal Distillery Cat- #theverbstheword, #kittysoze

Social Media
· Facebook- https://www.facebook.com/tenthwardco/
· Instagram- @tenthwardco
· Twitter- @tenthwardco
· Slogan- #wardoffordinary

Open Weds.–Sun. from 12–6. Tour $5. It is not necessary to book in advance.

Backstory: Tenth Ward Distilling Company forges offbeat spirits by experimenting with unconventional ingredients, recipes and aging techniques. We are dedicated to reviving Frederick's booze history in addition to providing distinctive tours, tastings and B.A.M.F. spirits.

The Grains: Rye, corn and barley for our distillery are grown down the road at Rippon Lodge Farm. Rusty (pictured) also malts our barley and rye and smokes our corn. Our cider, which is the base of our applejack (apple brandy aged in bourbon barrels), comes from McCutcheon's, a fourth-generation family-owned apple manufacturing plant that has been in Frederick since 1938. McCutcheon's sources all of their apples locally from Maryland, Virginia and Pennsylvania. Finally, our spring water from Catoctin Mountain is used to proof our whiskey.

Frederick distilling: Tenth Ward is the co-founder of the Frederick Area Distillery.

Association. For all inquiries related to the association, contact Monica Pearce at. monica@tenthwarddistilling.com or (30) 606-8645.

Maryland distilling: Tenth Ward is a member of the Maryland Distillers Guild. For all inquiries related to the guild, contact Kevin Atticks at kevin@growandfortify.com.

Photo ©Andrew Faulkner

Brandon & Tricia Egbert, Owner/Distiller
213 West Main Ave.
Ritzville, WA 99619
(509) 528-2297

Whiskeydistillery@gmail.com

Equipment: My distilling equipment was made by Affordable Equipment and cost just over $25,000. It consists of two 55-gallon Groen steam vessels for mashing or cooking corn, a 55-gallon four-plate still and a 55-gallon five-plate still.

Backstory: I own Whiskey Gap Distillery in a small farm town in the state of Washington. The town was called Whiskey Gap by rumrunners who, during Prohibition in the 1920s, brought alcohol from Canada to the city of Spokane.

I do everything myself. My wife and I do all the bottling by hand, sticking on each label one by one. I also sell my products in my little tasting room. I have been in business for about one year and five months, and recently one of my whiskeys won second place in Sip Northwest magazine's Best of the Northwest Spirits competition.

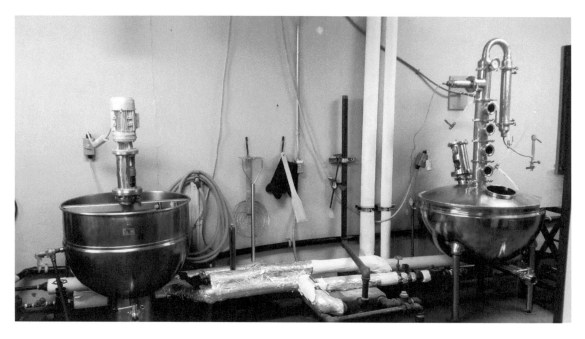

Great Notch Distillery

Randy Pratt

A sad day took place on July 31st, 2017. The Great Notch Distillery was officially and reluctantly closed by me. Not because my wife finally let me get a dog, or getting caught selling moonshine out of my trunk (I'm joking TTB, I know it's against the law), or anything tragically happening (divorce, explosion, bad bookkeeping), or falling out of love of distilling. It was simply two things—money and location.

I spoke of these two things in my story and they surely hold true. While the landlord situation seemed to have subsided after the changing of the locks there was the uncomfortable watchful and nosey eye of the landlord. This was stressful enough because I was trying to maintain a business and had to walk on egg shells in a unit I rented never feeling comfortable or wanted. There were days I simply dreaded going to the distillery when I saw the landlords car parked in the parking lot. This occurred at night and weekends, even holidays. There was always a knock on the door when I was focused on distilling numbers and proofing; a snoop around the inventory when bottling; an unneeded glance at a pipe that hasn't been used in twenty years just to get into the door. Then a million questions about the water and electric usage. "No, I didn't use 10,000 gallons of water as your water bill indicates". I would happily be jumping for joy if that was accurate because that would mean I had an outstanding sales quarter. As it turned out the lawn sprinkler system had sprung a leak and all the toilets were unnecessarily running. And, the new tenant he allowed into the complex used mega electricity to run his machines. The day I handed in the keys at the end of my lease there was a relief I wouldn't need to see this landlord again. I left the unit cleaner and in better shape than I had found it which helped keep his objections to a minimum.

The municipality would originally allow me to hold tours, tastings, and sell direct, then pulled the rug from under me after the State gave me permit approval. I met with the Mayor, Borough Attorney, Police Chief, Town Planner and Council Members "on my turf" at the distillery to plead my case that this is a unique and special opportunity in the town and the first in the County. Their reasoning was that if they allowed me to do a tour, have a tasting and sell directly to consumers what will prohibit the guy across the street from selling bumpers out of his auto body shop or someone opening a purse factory and sell purses from their building (their actual argument). Simply put, they could have made an exception and passed a resolution to allow ONLY the distillery to provide such a service at this specific address, but to no avail, I lost. I had a better shot at talking to one of my empty whiskey bottles; at least I would have enjoyed the drink.

There were whispers as to why the distillery wasn't allowed to progress because of local influences and contributions, none of which I want to go into here because they were just that—whispers. It's all whiskey under the bridge now.

Prior to the start of 2017 I was in an active search for a new location. I visited dozens of locations from rural farms to inner city industrial areas and when I crunched the numbers I couldn't financially have carried on (I certainly would have lost my wife). Having placed all my resources in the current location including plumbing and electrical upgrades, then calculating the needed upgrades, moving expenses, permits, etc. for a new location, it was a sad but responsible decision to close Great Notch Distillery. It was also a wise choice to keep my day job—and my wife.

I remain active in the distilling community, albeit from another view.

NANO-DISTILLERY STARTUP COST MODEL

Initial Capital/Fixed Assests	Est. Cost Range		Case Studies	
	Low	High	Lee Spirits, CO	Coastal Spirits, CA
60 gal still (with Electric Heat Elements)	$500.00	$6,000.00w	$4,300.00	$5,200.00
Gin Basket	$200.00	$1,500.00	$-	$250.00
Collection/Blending tanks	$250.00	$3,000.00	$850.00	$2,000.00
Explosion Proof Pneumatic Pump	$350.00	$1,000.00	$-	$400.00
Alcohol Tolerant Hoses, Fittings	$200.00	$1,000.00	$200.00	$200.00
Bottle Filler	$1,200.00	$2,500.00	$-	$1,800.00
Water filtration system (RO)	$300.00	$2,000.00	$100.00	$300.00
Product Filtration system				
Frame & Plate (20x20 cm)	$1,500.00	$2,500.00	$-	$1,900.00
Cartridge (10")	$500.00	$1,000.00	$-	$500.00
Stacker Lift				
New	$1,500.00	$5,000.00	$-	
Used	$500.00	$3,000.00	$-	$700.00
Air compressor (60 gal)	$300.00	$700.00	$100.00	$300.00
Labeler	$-	$2,000.00	$-	$1,800.00
Scale	$-	$2,500.00	$-	$-
Est. Total:	**$7,300.00**	**$33,700.00**	**$5,550.00**	**$15,350.00**
Contingency (~10%)	$730.00	$3,370.00	$555.00	$1,535.00
Fixed Asset Investment	**$8,030.00**	**$37,070.00**	**$6,105.00**	**$16,885.00**

Production Materials (COGS)	Est. Cost	
GNS (55 gal drum @ 190 prf)	$418.00	
Drum Shipping	$100.00	
Gin Botanicals	$209.00	
Bottles	$738.00	
Labels	$246.00	
Closures (Corks, shrink sleeves, $0.10 ea)	$49.20	
Shipper case w/ divider insert, label	$787.20	
Utility - Electricity + water	$40.00	
Federal Excise Tax ($2.70/PG, $0.43/btl)	$211.56	
Total:	**$2,798.96**	
Total cost $/Case (6 pack)	$34.13	
Total cost $/Drink	$0.36	

Revenue Comparison: Bottles vs. Drinks		
Initial proof gallons (1 x 55gal Drum @ 190PF)	104.5	
75% yield - proof gallons	78.38	
Total cases	82	
Total bottles	492	
Total drinks	7872	
PG per case (6pk 750ml at 40% abv [80prf])	0.954	
Drinks per case (16 1.5-oz drinks/btl x 6	96	
Revenue	**Per Drink**	**Per bottle**
Each	$10	$27
Total Revenue	$78,720.00	$13,284.00
Total Costs	$2,798.96	$2,798.96
Gross Profit	**$75,921.04**	**$10,485.04**
Profit Margin	**96%**	**79%**

CPSIA information can be obtained
at www.ICGtesting.com
Printed in the USA
BVHW020540160320
574848BV00012B/167